NOODLE SOUP RECIPES

A Highly Recommended Noodle Casserole Cookbook

(A Noodle Soup Cookbook You Will Need)

Argentina O'Brian

Published by Alex Howard

© **Argentina O'Brian**

All Rights Reserved

Noodle Soup Recipes: A Highly Recommended Noodle Casserole Cookbook (A Noodle Soup Cookbook You Will Need)

ISBN 978-1-990169-79-3

All rights reserved. No part of this guide may be reproduced in any form without permission in writing from the publisher except in the case of brief quotations embodied in critical articles or reviews.

Legal & Disclaimer

The information contained in this book is not designed to replace or take the place of any form of medicine or professional medical advice. The information in this book has been provided for educational and entertainment purposes only.

The information contained in this book has been compiled from sources deemed reliable, and it is accurate to the best of the Author's knowledge; however, the Author cannot guarantee its accuracy and validity and cannot be held liable for any errors or omissions. Changes are periodically made to this book. You must consult your doctor or get professional medical advice before using any of the suggested remedies, techniques, or information in this book.

Table of contents

Part 1 1
Introduction 2
What Is Gluten? 2
Why To Follow Gluten Free Diet 3
Gluten Free Breakfast Recipes 10
Rice Noodles With Eggs And Potatoes 10
Gluten Free Quinoa Noodles 12
Banana Waffles 13
Fruity French Toast Casserole 15
Fruity Bites 16
Gluten Free Lunch Recipes 18
Beef, Broccoli And Rice Noodle Stir Fry 20
Chicken, Vegetables And Rice Stir Fry 21
Prawns With Quinoa Noodles 22
Quinoa Noodles With Chiles 24
Gluten Free Dinner Recipes 26
Sesame Chicken 28
Battered Chicken Fry With Rice Noodles And Sweet And Sour Sauce 30
Quinoa Noodles With Spinach And Tomatoes 32
Rice Noodles With Vegetables And Beef 33
Chicken Delight 35
Beef, Eggs And Rice Noodles 37
Lemongrass And Quinoa Noodles Stir-Fry 39
Pork Stir Fry With Rice Noodles 40

Dinner Time Rice Noodles Salad 43
Snack Recipes 44
Baked Apples 44
Quinoa Power Bars 46
Kiwi Smoothie 47
Stuffed Mushrooms 48
Snack Time Bites 49
Mango Pudding 50
Rice Noodles And Potato Salad 52
Dry Fruit Rolls 53
Purple Pineapple Drink 54
Yogurt Popsicle 55
Soup Recipes 56
Rice Noodle Soup With Chicken 56
Thai Style Noodle Soup 58
Rice Noodles Soup With Lemon Chicken 59
Easy Noodles Soup Recipe 60
Quinoa Noodles Soup With Spinach And Meat 62
Sweet Potatoes And Rice Noodle Soup 63
Cabbage And Noodle Soup 65
Vermicelli Soup 66
Seafood Rice Noodle Soup 68
Pumpkin And Rice Noodle Soup 69
Appetizer Recipes 71
Coconut Noodle Soup 71
Mini Ham, Chesses And Noodles Cups 72
Vegetables And Quinoa Noodle Bites 74

Rice Noodles Salad 76

Vegetable Noodle Soup 77

Quinoa Noodle Appetizer Time Soup 78

Avocado And Rice Noodle Salads 80

Black Beans With Rice Noodles Appetizer 81

Eggplant And Rice Noodles 82

Meal Plans For 3 Weeks 83

Gluten Free Shopping List 86

Part 2 93

Introduction 94

Types Of Noodles & The Recipes 95

Udon Noodle Miso Soup 98

Peanut Udon Noodles 99

Thai Chicken Udon Soup 101

Spicy Udon Noodle Bowl 103

Yaki Udon 105

Lemongrass Chicken Udon 107

Meaty Kishimen Noodles 109

Udon With Grated Daikon & Beef 111

Carbonara Udon Noodles 112

Stir Fried Udon Noodles With Nori Seaweed Paste 114

Udon Noodles With Chilled Tomatoes 116

Creamy Curry Udon 117

Chili Chicken Ramen Noodles 120

Chicken Fajita Ramen Noodles 122

Cheesy Ramen Meat Pie 123

Italian Ramen Pizza Pie 125

Pineapple Meatballs Ramen 127
Teriyaki Chow Mein 129
Vegetable Ramen Soup 130
Ramen Pudding 132
Ramen Noodle Salad 134
Ramen Pad Thai 135
Thai Chicken Salad With Ramen Noodles 136
Broccoli And Ramen Noodle Salad 138
Ramen Beef Pie 140
Chicken Ramen Diablo 142
Fried Ice Cream Ramen 144
Raman Lasagna 146
Soba Noodles 148
Shrimp And Asparagus 148
Otsu 151
Cilantro Noodle Bowl 153
Ottolenghi Soba Noodles With Aubergine And Mango 155
Curried Noodle Patties 157
Cold Soba Noodles 159
Grilled Tofu & Soba Noodles 161
Almond Soba Noodles 163
Garlic Soba Noodles 165
Ginger Soba Noodles 167
Peanut Noodle Salad 169
Noodle Recipes 171
Simple Fried Noodles 171
Spicy Fried Noodles 173

Jawa Fried Noodle 175
Aceh Fried Noodle 177
Bandung Kocok Noodles 179
Celor Palembang Noodles 181
Bogor Soto Noodles 183
Cakalang Manado Noodles 185
Bangka Chicken Noodles 187
Bangka Koba Noodles 189

Part 1

Introduction

If you love your noodles, pasta, or any baked stuff, but a medical condition makes you gluten intolerant, then you are in right place. Being gluten-challenged is not fun. Some of our best meals and comfort foods are usually made with gluten-containing grains. Breaking up with wheat noodles can be hard to do.
But – help is at hand.
This cookbook covers some of the finest and the most delicious gluten-free noodle recipes available today. While most of the recipes in this book are noodle-based, a small number use other forms of two great mainstays of gluten-free cooking, rice and quinoa.
Although there are some tests for gluten sensitivity, many people whose health improves on a gluten-free diet do not meet criteria for a formal medical diagnosis of celiac disease or even gluten intolerance. But, for the growing number of people who discover that avoid wheat, rye, and barley makes a noticeable difference for them, this book will be helpful.
This whole approach to meal planning is not really a "diet," but more a lifestyle change. Let's start with some basics, for instance - what is gluten?

What Is Gluten?

Gluten is a protein found in some specific food items. It is been used as a binding agent to add stickiness and elasticity to doughs. You find gluten mostly in cereal grains, especially in wheat, rye, and barley. Some food-sensitive individuals can have a problem with one of those grains but not others, but most of the time, a gluten-intolerant person needs to avoid all of them.
Scientifically, gluten composed of two proteins namely gliadin and glutenin. In the intestines, we can also digest gluten down into morphine like natural materials called exorphins.

Why To Follow Gluten Free Diet

For someone with gluten sensitivity or intolerance, eating foods containing gluten will cause inflammation in the intestines. In many cases, this condition gets a disease label known as celiac disease. But, you don't have to have a celiac disease diagnosis to need to avoid gluten.
The effect of gluten inside the intestine can not only cause pain and digestive problems, but also a "leaky gut" that lets large allergy-causing proteins from partially digested foods of other types into the bloodstream to trigger even more damage and symptoms all over.
If you are consuming gluten and experience fatigue, joint pain, or diarrhea then you may be one of the legions of people for whom a better diet is a surprising

answer that avoids dangerous drug treatments and ongoing misery.

Stress no more, as we give you a basic gluten free diet plan along with 50 simple, easy to cook gluten free recipes to get you healthy again.

Anyone can follow this diet. To make the process smoother, here are some listed benefits of the diet.

A gluten free diet is a popular phrase in recent years, but it is likely here to stay. In the end, grains like wheat are a specialized type of grass. Are you allergic to ordinary grasses?

Our bodies were not made to eat wheat every day. They can be allergic or intolerant to anything we eat – and for whatever reasons, this is especially true for gluten-containing grains. Rice is also a grain, but for whatever complex reasons, it is typically easier for people with gluten intolerances to eat without problems.

Rice, especially brown rice, and quinoa are better-tolerated, healthier types of grains. The advantage of quinoa in particular is that it brings you a lot of protein compared with other types of carbohydrate-containing foods.

The common benefits of this eating style for you might include:

- Improving gastrointestinal problems

- Preventing and reducing bloating
- Getting rid of frequent headaches, fatigue and pain.
- Reducing the symptoms of constipation
- Providing more energy, sense of well-being, and better overall health

With just a little extra planning and creativity in cooking and food choices, you can enjoy most foods. Gluten-free food makers (and even restaurants) have gotten better and better at developing tasty alternatives for you.

Mainstream supermarkets have special gluten-free items available – you don't even have to find a health food store for many common recipe ingredients or prepared items. Finding good substitutes for the gluten-containing foods is very possible.

To help you out, here is the list of food items that are been allowed, as well as exclude in gluten free diet.

Food list of allowed and not allowed items for a gluten free lifestyle

Allowed

- Beans
- Poultry (not breaded)
- Fruits
- Fresh meats

- Soy
- Millet
- Nuts (unprocessed form)
- Fresh organic eggs
- Fresh fish
- Seeds
- Vegetables
- Dairy products
- Arrowroot
- Rice
- Tapioca
- Flax
- Amaranth
- Corn and cornmeal
- Gluten free rice flours
- Corn
- Quinoa
- Buckwheat
- Sorghum

Not Allowed

- Bulgur
- Kamut

- Semolina
- Graham flour
- Barley
- Rye
- Spelt
- Durum flour
- Farina
- Wheat (plain and self-rising)
- Triticale

Picking up the Most Suitable Food Items

Whenever you buy any food item, make sure that you read the label thoroughly. Scan the ingredient lists for hidden gluten contents. So watch for all the items that may contain gluten. In the U.S., manufacturers will tell you if a food is made in a plant that also processes other foods to which allergic people might have a reaction.

Oatmeal is a whole debate in the gluten-free world unto itself. There are brands of oatmeal made in gluten-free processing plants. Some people do and others don't react adversely to oats. As with most food-related problems, your ultimate criterion is to test each single food by itself and see if it causes symptoms or not.

Go for gluten free, organic and fresh products. Sometimes gluten sneaks into packaged foods and condiments where you might not suspect.

Why Choose Quinoa Noodles or Rice Noodles for Most of These Recipes?

Both quinoa and rice are high in protein and other amino acids. Both of these ingredients are excellent source of iron, phosphorus, protein, magnesium. These ingredients are part of a balanced diet that lends itself to vegan or vegetarian style of cooking, as well as to cooking with chicken, fish, or meats.

Rice and quinoa noodles are great in texture and taste. One of the important parts of adapting smoothly to a gluten-free lifestyle is enjoying favorite foods without needing to eat wheat. Both quinoa and rice are inexpensive and easily available in grocery stores.

One of several highly recommended brands of organic gluten-free brown rice noodle products is Jovial.® You want a noodle that has both good texture and taste after cooking as well as in combination with various sauces and seasonings.

Although this recipe book does not focus on gluten-free comfort foods, just ease your mind. You do not have to deprive yourself. Realize that you can always enjoy your old favorites of mac and cheese or spaghetti and meatballs. Just make those dishes with rice or quinoa noodles instead of wheat noodles. You can even find relatively healthy gluten-free versions of these meals in the freezer case at your grocery or health food store. Heat in a microwave for a few minutes and you have a quick and easy gluten free comfort food meal whenever you need one.

Gluten Free Breakfast Recipes

Breakfast needs to be light and healthy. This is the most important meal of the day, not a meal to skip because of being too busy or tired or rushed. These recipes are as do-able as anything similar in the gluten-containing meal world.

Rice Noodles With Eggs And Potatoes

For some people, breakfasts are not complete without eggs. Most people love eggs, unless they are allergic to them. They are quick and easy to make and are rich in protein, vitamins and minerals. Experts have recently decided that eggs are OK for you because of their nutritional value. You have the option of buying organic and higher omega 3 containing eggs that may cut down on some of the less desirable aspects of eating commercial eggs.
We will make this gluten free breakfast with some low calorie ingredients. You will love the taste of this recipe. Moreover, the potatoes offer just the perfect amount of carbs to start the day with energy to fuel your body without gluten.

Preparation time: 15 minutes
Yield 3-4 servings

Ingredients

4 tablespoons of olive oil
2 garlic cloves
2 small onion, chopped
1 zucchini, sliced
2 red bell peppers, chopped
4 eggs
1 cup white potatoes, cut in small cubes and boiled
½ cup mushrooms chopped
1 cup rice noodles
Salt, paprika and black pepper, to taste

Preparation

- Heat olive oil in a skillet and sauté the onions along with garlic
- Next, add zucchini, bell pepper, mushrooms, potatoes and cook until the ingredients become tender
- Now beat the eggs in small bowl and pour on to the vegetables
- Sprinkle salt, pepper and paprika on top
- Give it a stir for even cooking, once eggs are cooked turn off the heat
- Place the rice noodles in the bowl and pour the prepared mixture on top
- Serve and enjoy this mouth-watering breakfast.

Gluten Free Quinoa Noodles

All of the ingredients are readily available. This dish cooks up in just a few minutes. The quinoa noodles provide an energy boost to start your day.

Preparation time: 15 minutes
Cooking time: 25-30minutes
Yield: 6 servings

Ingredients

1 packet quinoa noodles, cooked and drained
1 and half large cup water
½ cup quinoa flakes
½ cup peaches, chopped
½ cup walnuts, chopped
½ cup dates, pitted and chopped
6 tablespoons of agave nectar

Preparation

- Heat olive oil in a pan and sauté the onions
- Place quinoa noodles in a bowl and add peaches, dates, water, walnuts and nectar of agave
- Transfer this mixture into the pan and cook for about 15 minutes
- Once the texture gets fluffy, stir it and serve in a bowl to enjoy this gluten free breakfast.

Banana Waffles

Who says that you cannot enjoy something special? This is a perfect sweet breakfast recipe that will please the whole family. Everyone loves waffles. Add any type of your favorite fruit in chunks. For this version, we are making it with creamy bananas, which are sweet, but full of potassium and other valuable nutrients.

Preparation time: 15 minutes
Cooking time: 10 minutes
Yield: 2 -4 servings

Ingredients

4 large bananas, mashed
½ cups rice milk
6 tablespoons of almond oil
4 tablespoon raw honey, or as per taste
3 cups gluten free rice flour
2 teaspoons baking powder
Pinch of salt
1 cup walnuts

Tools Needed: Waffle iron

Preheat the waffle iron, before starting the cooking process.

Preparation

- Take an electric blender and blend bananas, oil, honey and milk
- Next, pour in the flour, salt and baking soda
- At the end, fold in the walnuts
- Combine all the ingredients well and then pour into greased and preheated waffle iron
- Let bake for about 10 minutes and then serve with your favorite fruit toppings or with honey on top
- Serve and enjoy.

Fruity French Toast Casserole

This French toast recipe is a perfect gluten free delight, which can fill the "void" of avoiding wheat bread on a gluten free menu program.

Preparation time: 15 minutes
Cooking time: 30 minutes
Yield: 4 serving

Ingredients

½ loaf gluten-free bread, cut into 2-inch cubes
¾ cup frozen or fresh blueberries (depending on the season)
6 large eggs
2 cups coconut milk
1 cup honey
½ teaspoon ground cinnamon
½ tablespoon vanilla extract

Preparation

- Take a large baking dish and place the cubed bread and blueberries in it
- Whisk eggs in a separate bowl
- Take a medium bowl and combine eggs mix, coconut milk, honey, cinnamon and vanilla

- Pour the mixture over the bread and blueberries in the baking dish
- Bake in oven at 375 degree F for about 30 minutes
- Once done, serve and enjoy.

Fruity Bites

If you are on gluten free diet and does not want to add oats to your meals, then this recipe gives you an alternative based on quinoa, with some sweet fruit combinations. Once you take a bite, you will want more.

Preparation time: 10 minutes
Cooking time: 20 minutes
Yield: 4 servings

Ingredients

2 cups cooked quinoa
1 teaspoon cinnamon
1 teaspoon nutmeg
6 tablespoons brown sugar
1 tablespoon honey
1 cup chopped apples
4 eggs, beaten
6 tablespoons almond flour (just crush the almonds to make the flour)

Preparation

- Preheat the oven at 375 degree F
- Take bowl and add cooked quinoa
- In a separate bowl, combine all the remaining listed ingredients
- Combine ingredients of both bowls
- Now take a muffin tray and place muffin paper into each muffin cup
- Bake in the oven for about 20 minutes
- Once the bites overflow, they are ready to be served
- Tip: Best served warm

Gluten Free Lunch Recipes

Lunch is the second most important meal of the day. After a busy morning, you need to reboot your energy reserves with more gluten-free choices. This high protein carbohydrate food is a great option.

Peanut and Sesame Rice Noodles

This is a perfect lunchtime recipe that is chewy and crunchy at the same time. The peanut adds a favorite classic flavor and nuttiness to this recipe. It is prepared in a few minutes, yet tastes delicious.

Preparation time: 10 minutes
Yield: 4 servings

Ingredients

2 green onions, thinly sliced or chopped
½ cup broccoli slaw
1 cup unsalted peanuts , chopped
100 grams rice noodles
½ cup sesame oil
1 tomato, chopped
1/2 block extra firm tofu (pressed and cubed)

Preparation

In a large bowl, combine all of the listed ingredients. Once all the ingredients are coated well with the oil and seasonings, serve onto plates and enjoy.

Beef, Broccoli And Rice Noodle Stir Fry

For the meat lover out there, this recipe is for you.

Cook Time: 15 Minutes
Yield 4 servings

Ingredients

1 pound beef
4 garlic cloves, smashed
2 tablespoons minced fresh ginger
1-1/2 bunch broccoli
4 tablespoons olive oil
½ cup water
1 cup beef broth
150-200 grams rice noodles, cooked

Preparation

- In a bowl add beef, ginger and garlic and let it stand for few minutes.
- In a cooking pan, add oil and cook broccoli in it over high heat.
- Add the water to the pan, cook for 2 minutes and then transfer the broccoli to a plate.
- Now add oil to same pan and add the beef mixture. Cook for about 5 minutes. Add in broth.

- Once the gravy formed, add the broccoli mix and cook for additional 5 minutes
- Serve this gravy over rice noodles and enjoy.

Chicken, Vegetables And Rice Stir Fry

This is a quick and delicious recipe full of iron, protein, carbohydrates, sodium, and healthy minerals.

Cooking time: 15 minutes
Yield: 5 servings

Ingredients

2 cups brown rice, boiled
4 teaspoons sunflower oil
4 chicken breast fillets, sliced
2 large carrots, peeled and thinly sliced
150 g snow peas, ends trimmed, thinly sliced
1 cup honey

Preparation

- Take a frying pan and heat oil in it. Add in the chicken and stir-fry for about 3 minutes
- Transfer it to a bowl. If any chicken remains, cook until all the chicken is fried

- To the same pan, add the carrots and peas. Cook for about 2 minutes
- Return the chicken to the pan and cook along with the vegetables for one more minute
- Now add honey and soy sauce and stir-fry for one minute
- Layer the brown rice on a plate and top with the prepared gravy.

Prawns With Quinoa Noodles

With some great flavors and perfect aroma, you can prepare this recipe in a few minutes. It is a perfect stir-fry dish to enjoy at lunchtime.

Preparation time: 5 minutes
Cooking time: 10 minutes
Yield: 6 servings

Ingredients

4 tablespoons olive oil
2 eggs, beaten
250 grams prawns, peeled and cooked
150 grams gluten-free flavor sauce (check out Asian or sesame ginger flavoring)
40 grams peanuts, dry roasted and chopped
2 bunch spring onions, thinly sliced

200 grams quinoa noodles, cooked and drained
Lemon wedges for garnishing
Salt, to taste

Preparation

- Heat half of the oil in a frying pan and add eggs to make a scramble. Remove once done and set this aside for a while.
- Heat the remaining oil and add onions to sauté
- Add prawns and sauce. Simmer for about 2 minutes and then, add peanuts.
- Now place the scramble eggs in the cooking pan and add noodles.
- Toss the mixture well for evenly coating
- Just before serving garnish with lemon wedges.
- Sprinkle salt as seasoning as per liking.
- Enjoy

Quinoa Noodles With Chiles

It is a perfect recipe to serve on cold days. The roasted chili and quinoa noodles combine well with lots of flavor and aromas from the seasonings and vegetables.

Preparation time: 25 minutes
Cooking time: 20 minutes
Yield: 6 servings

Ingredients

1 red bell pepper
1 poblano chiles
6 teaspoons olive oil
2 cups chopped zucchini
2 cups chopped onion
6 garlic cloves, minced
½ tablespoon chili powder
½ teaspoon ground cumin
1 teaspoon paprika
1 cup water

1-2 cups uncooked quinoa, rinsed
Pinch of salt
1 cup diced tomatoes
1 cup pinto beans, rinsed and drained
1 cup vegetable broth

Preparation

- Preheat the boiler.
- Meanwhile, cut the chiles lengthwise and discard seeds.
- Then place on boiler, once blackened set aside for a while and then chopped
- Take a pan and heat oil in it
- Then add peppers, chiles, and water.
- Add the remaining list of ingredients and then bring it to boil
- Cover the pan and cook for 20 minutes so that the ingredients simmer
- Serve over the cooked quinoa noodles. Enjoy!

Gluten Free Dinner Recipes

Dinner is the time when all family members can join together for a delicious meal. Here are some simple quick recipes for you.

Vegetable Noodles Stir-Fry

Looking for something meatless? Then try this vegan noodle recipe. The Chinese chiles simply give a perfect kick to the overall flavor of this recipe.

Preparation time: 15 minutes
Yield: 4 servings

Ingredients

8 ounces rice noodles, cooked and drained
2 tablespoons olive oil
6 ounces mushrooms, sliced
4 cloves of garlic, minced
4 green onions, sliced
½ cup soy sauce
2 tablespoons brown sugar
1 tablespoon lime juice
2 tablespoons sesame oil
2 tablespoons ketchup
1 tablespoon black beans paste

1 teaspoon Chinese chiles
3 large eggs
3 cups baby spinach

Preparation

- Heat oil in a skillet, add mushrooms and sauté for about 5 minutes.
- Next, add in garlic and onions and cook for about two additional minutes.
- In a bowl combine soy sauce, brown sugar, lime juice, sesame oil, ketchup, black bean paste, Chinese chiles
- Pour the mixture into the skillet and cook for one minute
- Then add spinach and add eggs to make a scramble.
- Cook for additional one minute and then toss the noodles.
- Stir well for fine coating
- Enjoy

Sesame Chicken

This is the best chicken recipe that is prepared with just a few simple ingredients. Serve the chicken with boiled rice for a full-bodied meal.

Preparation time: 20 minutes
Yield: 6 servings

Ingredients

2 lbs of chicken tenders cut in to bite-sized pieces
4 Tablespoons of rice vinegar
2 cups chicken broth, homemade
½ cup sugar
1 cup cornstarch + 6 teaspoons water mix together to form a paste
1 tablespoon of cornstarch
4 egg whites, lightly beaten
1 cup olive oil
2 teaspoon garlic, minced
8 dried hot pepper pods
½ cup sesame seeds
1 green onions, chopped
Cooked jasmine rice, as needed per # of servings
4 tablespoons gluten-free soy sauce
Salt and pepper to taste

Preparation

- Take a bowl and combine sugar, half of the vinegar, 2 tablespoons soy sauce and half of the chicken broth
- In another bowl, combine chicken pieces along with remaining broth, soy sauce and vinegar.
- Leave the chicken marinating for about 20 minutes
- Afterward add egg whites and 1 tablespoon of cornstarch.
- Combine well so the ingredients coat the chicken
- In a wok, heat the oil and cook the chicken in it. Once golden brown remove and drain on paper towels.
- Now in same wok, add garlic and sauté.
- Then add sesame seeds and the cornstarch already dissolved in water.
- You can add salt and pepper to taste
- Once the bubbly sauce made, add the chicken and top it with green onions
- Serve with boiled rice

Battered Chicken Fry With Rice Noodles And Sweet And Sour Sauce

It is a perfect Chinese chicken recipe, for all celiac and gluten-intolerance sufferers. It is simply delicious to eat and also goes well with soy sauce and quinoa noodles

Preparation time: 15 minutes

Yield: 6 servings

Ingredients

500 grams chicken
Salt and pepper to taste
100 g rice flour
1 tablespoon corn flour
1 teaspoons of baking powder
2 eggs, beaten
150 ml of cold water
Gluten-free sweet and sour sauce, to taste
4 cups rice noodles, boiled and drained

Preparation

- In a small bowl, combine all of the dry ingredients including salt, pepper, corn flour, rice flour, baking powder
- Next, add eggs and gently stir to combine all the ingredients to form a paste

- The add in cold water to make the mixture runny
- Now add chicken to the bowl and mix to coat the chicken well
- Next, in a non-stick pan, heat the oil and fry the chicken pieces.
- Once golden brown, take them out.
- In a separate bowl, heat the sweet and sour sauce. Now place the chicken pieces over the noodles and drizzle hot sweet and sour sauce on top.
- Enjoy.

Quinoa Noodles With Spinach And Tomatoes

Here is another great recipe to keep your taste buds happy.

Preparation time: 20 minutes
Yield: 6 servings

Ingredients

10 ounces quinoa noodles
4 tablespoons olive oil
4 garlic cloves, ground
12 ounces cherry tomatoes
10 ounces packages baby spinach
8 tablespoons Parmesan cheese, finely grated and divided
4 teaspoons chopped fresh marjoram, divided
1 teaspoon red pepper, dried and crushed
Salt and pepper for sprinkling, to taste

Preparation

- Cook the noodles according to package instruction, drain and set aside
- Reserve just ½ cup of pasta liquid
- Now heat oil in a pan and add tomatoes, salt and pepper
- Add the garlic and cook for 30 seconds

- Now add the reserved pasta liquid into the rest of the mix.
- Next, add in spinach and marjoram, along with pepper
- Once the spinach wilts, add cheese and noodles in the pan and cook until all the liquid drains, for about 2 minutes
- Serve and enjoy.

Rice Noodles With Vegetables And Beef

A perfect gluten-free rice noodle dish that combines simple ingredients to make a dish that serves the whole family. It adds a new flavor twist or innovation to how you prepare this meal.

Preparation time: 15 minutes
Yield: 6 servings

Ingredients:

1 package rice noodles, cooked and drained
1.5 pounds beef steak, cooked medium rare
½ pound snow peas, stem removed
3 large shallots, thinly sliced a, rings form
6 garlic cloves, chopped
2 scallions, finely chopped

1/4 cup cilantro
1 teaspoon lime zest, finely grated + 2 tablespoons lime juice
Salt and ground pepper, to taste
2 teaspoons honey

Preparation

- Heat oil in skillet and add in steak already seasoned with salt and pepper
- Cook 2 to 6 minutes per side for medium rare cooking.
- Once cooked transfer the steak to wooden board and cut in pieces.
- Add in same skillet the garlic, shallots and cook for about one minute
- Now add the limejuice, lime zest, honey, and water and cook to form gravy.
- Next, add snow peas and cook for additional 4 minutes, tossing occasionally, until tender, but crisp.
- Add noodles and stir twice
- Top with slices of steak and remaining juices in skillet.
- Top with cilantro, serve, and enjoy.

Chicken Delight

This is a rich textured recipe, with great taste and divine flavors.

Cooking time: 15 minutes
Yield 3 servings

Ingredients

1 cup chicken pieces, boiled
1 cup boiled rice noodles
1 cup sweet potatoes
½ teaspoon chili sauce
½ tablespoon soy sauce
½ teaspoon salt
1 teaspoon pepper
½ teaspoon red chiles
4 tablespoon vegetable oil

Preparation

- In a frying pan heat oil and add in chicken pieces, cook until brown
- Add sweet potatoes and cook for 2 minutes.
- Add in boiled rice noodles.
- Sprinkle salt, pepper, red chiles, and soy sauce, chili sauce

- Stir twice and serve instantly
- Enjoy

Beef, Eggs And Rice Noodles

A dinnertime hit recipe that combines the hit flavors of meat, rice and eggs. Perfect dinner for each family member.

Preparation time: 20 minutes
Yield 3 servings

Ingredients

1 cup beef, thin pieces
2 cups cooked rice noodles, drained
5 tablespoons water
1-2 organic eggs, whisked
2 tablespoons gluten-free soy sauce
½ teaspoon salt
½ teaspoon black pepper
½ teaspoon Chinese salt
Olive oil for frying

Preparation

- Take a frying pan and heat oil in it, add beef pieces and cook for about 10 minutes.
- Add in a little amount of water so that the meat cooks properly
- Then add whisked eggs and cook for an additional 5 minutes.

- Once the beef cooked thoroughly add in the rice and sprinkle salt, Chinese salt and black pepper
- At the end, pour on the soy sauce

Lemongrass And Quinoa Noodles Stir-Fry

Lemon grass is the most important ingredient in this recipe that lends its aromatic flavor and divine taste. Once you taste it, you will ask for more.

Cooking time: 10 minutes
Yield 4 servings

Ingredients

1/2 cup peanut oil
600g beef sirloin, thinly sliced
2 onion, thinly sliced
2 yellow capsicum, thinly sliced
1 clove garlic, crushed
1 stalks lemongrass, trimmed
2 long red chiles, thinly sliced
1tablespoons soy sauce
2 tablespoons fish sauce
2 cups quinoa noodles, to serve

Preparation

- Heat oil in a pan and add oil, and swirl
- Add half of the beef and cook for 4 minutes for frying.
- Remove it and dish out in plate, set aside.

- Add more oil to pan and cook remaining beef. Cook and set aside
- Now sauté onions, garlic, capsicum in oil and add lemongrass and chiles as well.
- Stir-fry for 5 minutes and then add all the cooked beef.
- Add soy sauce and fish sauce and serve with quinoa noodles.

Pork Stir Fry With Rice Noodles

You probably have never made pork tenderloin so quickly before. Serve this delicious recipe at dinnertime for mouthwatering pleasure.

Cooking time: 25 minutes
Yield 2 servings

Ingredients

250g pork tenderloin
1 tablespoon hoisin sauce
150g dried thin rice noodles
2 tablespoons peanut oil
5 garlic cloves, thinly sliced
2 tablespoon ginger, thinly sliced
½ bunch broccolini, trimmed
4 spring onions cut into 6cm lengths

100g sugar snap peas, trimmed
½ bunch Choy sum, trimmed (substitute bok choy if choy sum not available)
1 tablespoon of dark gluten-free soy sauce
1-teaspoon sesame oil
Salt and pepper to taste

Preparation

- Preheat oven at 375 degree F.
- Take a baking pan and place liner on it.
- Place the pork on flat plate and brush sauce and season with pepper and salt.
- Now place pork for roasting in baking pan in to oven. Once the pork is brown, remove from oven and let it rest for a while.
- Cook noodles according to package instructions. Drain excess water and set aside.
- In a large frying pan heat peanut oil and stir-fry garlic and ginger
- Add broccolini and spring onions.
- Add cold water and increase heat
- Add sugar and Choy and cook for 3 minutes.
- Add soy sauce and pour in the sesame oil.
- In a dish, layer noodles and place slice on pork on the side.

- Pour the prepared vegetable mixture on top and at the end, sprinkle sesame oil on top.

Dinner Time Rice Noodles Salad

Here you have a light and delicious salad to serve at dinnertime. This is a simple healthy recipe for dinner.

Preparation time: 5 minutes
Yield: 4 servings

Ingredients

 5 cloves garlic, minced
1 cup chopped cilantro
1 jalapeno
3 tablespoons lime juice
15 ounce rice noodles
4 carrots
1 cup peanuts
1 spring mint

Preparation

- Cook the rice noodles per package instructions
- Combine all the listed ingredients in a bowl and toss well.
- Serve and enjoy

Snack Recipes

Baked Apples

This recipe is fruity, delicious and gluten-free at the same time. The ingredients bring you iron, protein, vitamins, and other essential nutrients. Simple organic dessert recipe to enjoy

Preparation time: 10 minutes
Cooking time: 25 minutes
Yield 3 servings

Ingredients

3 organic apples, center cored
½ cup raisins
½ cup walnuts
½ cup honey

Preparation

- Preheat oven at 375 degree F
- In a bowl, combine honey, walnuts and raisins
- Now peeled the apples and center cored them
- Now place the mixture in center-cored apples and bake in oven for about 20-25 minutes
- Once baked serve and enjoy

Quinoa Power Bars

Here is a hearty dessert treat to enjoy at any time.

Preparation time: 10 minutes
Cooking time: 20 minutes
Yield: 4 servings
Ingredients

1 cup almond flour
1 cup quinoa flakes cooked
4 tablespoons flax seed meal
4 tablespoons sugar
4 eggs
1 tablespoon raisins

Preparation

- Take a bowl and combine all the listed ingredients
- Pour this mixture into the baking dish and bake for 20 minutes

- Serve by cutting into bars and enjoy

Kiwi Smoothie

Kiwi is a fruit full of carbohydrates and other minerals. It is a perfect light gluten-free drink that can be enjoyed as little sweet treat.

Preparation time: 5 minutes
Yield 2 servings

Ingredients

2 cup kiwi, cut in cubes
2 mint leaves
2 cup coconut milk
Ice cubes, for chilling
6 tablespoons honey
Preparation

- Take a blender and pour all ingredients in it.
- Blend until smooth.
- Serve in tall glasses and enjoy.
- For a chilled drink, serve with ice cubes

Stuffed Mushrooms

This reliable standby is a great appetizer that you can stuff with potatoes or other foods of choice for a great mix of flavors and texture.

Preparation time: 5 minutes
Cooking time: 20 minutes
Total time: 25 minutes

Ingredients

4 potatoes, peeled and boiled
3 cup mushrooms
Salt and black pepper to taste

Preparation

- Combine boiled potatoes, salt and pepper in a bowl and stuff the mushroom caps with the mixture
- Bake in oven at 375 degree F for 15 minutes
- Once done serve and enjoy.

Snack Time Bites

This recipe yields about 24 bites. You make it in a muffin tray that gives it a creative look. Serve and enjoy this little snack any time with your favorite dipping sauce. A perfect gluten-free snack for all celiac sufferers.

Yield: 24 bites
Cooking time: 20 minutes

Ingredients

2 cups cooked quinoa, cooled slightly, drained and cooled
2 organic eggs
3 egg whites
2 cups pepperoni
2 cups black olives
2 cups pineapple, cubed
2 cups ham, cooked and shredded in small pieces
2 cups onions
Salt and black pepper taste
1 cup cottage cheese, organic
2 cups rice noodles, cooked

Preparation

- Line the muffin tray with muffin shaped parchment paper.
- Combine all the listed ingredients in a bowl
- Fill the muffin tray with the mixture and bake in oven at 300 degree F for 20 minutes
- Once done, take them out and let it cool
- Serve with your favorite dipping sauce.

Mango Pudding

A delicious and fruity snack time sweet, that satisfies your craving for dessert.

Cooking time: 4 hours (for overnight chilling)
Serves: 7 servings

Ingredients

4 mangoes (peeled and cubed)
2 cups water
1 cup sugar
1 cup whipping cream
1 tablespoons corn-starch
¼ tablespoons water

Preparation

- Combine the chopped mangoes and ¼ of the water in a blender
- Combine until smooth
- Discard any solid.
- Now add remaining water at a medium heat and add sugar to the pan. Cook until dissolved
- Add the mango puree and stir with the whisk
- Pour the cornstarch mixture in it and cook until thick
- Next, place the mixture in the bowl and chill overnight in freezer
- Finally, place cream in the bowl and then whisk until foamy.
- Serve with frozen dessert

Rice Noodles And Potato Salad

A carbohydrate rich snack to enjoy at dinnertime.

Preparation time: 10 minutes
Yield: 6servings

Ingredients

8 large organic potatoes, boiled
4 large onion, minced
4 large carrot, diced
2cup celery, diced
5 tablespoons minced dill
3 cup mayonnaise
1 tablespoons vinegar
2 cup rice noodles, cooked

Preparation

- Combine all the listed ingredients in bowl and serve
- Enjoy.

Dry Fruit Rolls

A classic snack full of nutrients and energy. This is made without gluten, but it is creamy and great tasting.

Preparation time: 5 minutes
Total time: 20 minutes

Ingredients

½ cup apricots, dried
½ cup dried dates, soft versions
1 cup of cherries, dried
2 tablespoon of coconut oil
4 tablespoon of sesame seed

Preparation

- In a food processor, puree the dates along with cherries, apricots, coconut oil
- Once a thick texture forms, transfer to a plate and then make balls by hand
- Coat with sesame seeds, then serve and enjoy.

Purple Pineapple Drink

To please all the smoothie lovers out there, this is a bonus recipe and perfect gluten-free smoothie to get you going any time of the day.

Preparation time: 5 minutes
Yield: 4 servings

Ingredients

4 cups soymilk (or use rice or almond milk alternatives, as desired)
½ cup blueberries
4 bananas, peeled and chopped
2 cups pineapple juice

Preparation

- Combine all the listed ingredients in blender and once smooth serve in to glasses filled with ice cubes
- Enjoy.

Yogurt Popsicle

To make a healthier gluten-free treat, this homemade popsicle is a great way to get healthy fruits and calcium into your kids without a fight.

Yield: 4 servings
Freeze overnight

Ingredients

4 small ripe bananas
2 cup frozen blueberries
6 cups non-fat plain yogurt
6 tablespoons honey

Preparation

- Combine all the ingredients in a blender and blend until smooth
- Pour the mixture into popsicle molds and freeze overnight
- Serve and enjoy.

Soup Recipes

Rice Noodle Soup With Chicken

If you are cutting calories and gluten from your diet, then this recipe is what you need. This soup is full of flavor, low in calories and high in nutrition.

Preparation time: 15 minutes
Yield: 4 servings

Ingredients

1 ounce rice noodles
10 ounces chicken breasts, boneless and skinless
2 tablespoon peanut oil
4 teaspoons minced garlic
1 teaspoons minced ginger
½ teaspoon red pepper flakes
30 ounces chicken broth
4 tablespoons fish sauce
1 tablespoon fresh cilantro , chopped

4 tablespoons green onions , chopped
1 tablespoon fresh basil , chopped

Preparation

- Prepare noodles according to package instructions.
- Meanwhile cut the chicken in to julienne strips and heat oil in pan.
- Cook the chicken until brown, then add garlic, ginger and pepper flakes
- Cook for about one minute, and then add fish sauce and broth.
- Bring the mixture to the boil and cook for about 10 minute.
- Now drain the noodle and cut in to small pieces.
- Then add noodles into the serving bowl and ladle the soup on the top.
- Sprinkle cilantro, onion and basil on top.
- Serve and enjoy.

Thai Style Noodle Soup

If you have not yet tried rice noodles in soup before, then you should give this recipe a try. It is a simple and mouth-watering soup recipe made easily in just 15 minutes.

Preparation time: 15 minutes
Yield: 5 servings

Ingredients

1 cup water
6 cups chicken stock
1 package rice noodles, cooked
8 ounces chicken, thinly sliced
2 cups mushroom, sliced
1 cups spinach
4 tablespoons fish sauce

Preparation

- In cooking pot, bring water along with water and chicken stock to boil
- Add the mushrooms and then simmer
- Then add chicken pieces and cook until chicken becomes moist and tender
- Now add spinach and next, the fish sauce.

- Cook for a few more minutes
- Place the rice noodles in a serving bowl and then pour the soup over it
- Serve hot and enjoy.

Rice Noodles Soup With Lemon Chicken

Hot, tangy and delicious soup to make, especially when on gluten free diet

Preparation time: 15-20 minutes
Yield: 4 servings

Ingredients

2/3 tablespoon olive oil
1 1/3 cups sliced carrots
1 1/3 cups sliced celery
1/3 cup chopped onion
8 cups chicken broth
2/3 lb chopped boneless skinless chicken breast (raw or cooked)
1 cup quinoa noodles, cooked and rinsed
4 tablespoons lemon juice (about 3 lemons)
1/3 teaspoon ground black pepper
2 2/3 cups chopped fresh Baby Spinach

Preparation

- Take a large cooking pot and heat olive oil in it.
- Cook carrots, celery and onion in olive oil for about 20 minutes
- Add chicken broth, lemon juice, chicken, quinoa and pepper
- Bring the mixture to a boil and then add spinach
- Cook until tender.
- Add spinach and cook until tender.
- At the end, add noodles and serve by sprinkling spinach.

Easy Noodles Soup Recipe

A simple and delicious soup ready in just a few minutes with simple and readily available ingredients.

Preparation time: 20 minutes
Yield: 4 servings

Ingredients

2/3 tablespoons olive oil
1/3 cup onions, chopped
1/3 cup celery, chopped
1 garlic clove, minced

5 cans chicken broth
2 can vegetable broth
1 lb chopped cooked chicken breast, shredded
1 cup quinoa noodles , cooked
1/3 cup carrot , sliced
1 teaspoon dried basil
2/3 teaspoon dried oregano
salt and pepper, to taste

Preparation

- In a pot, heat oil and cook onions, celery, garlic and carrots
- Add in broth and chicken pieces and cook for 5 minutes
- Now add noodles, basil, oregano salt and pepper
- Bring the mixture to boil and then serve

Quinoa Noodles Soup With Spinach And Meat

A perfect gluten free hearty soup to make and enjoy.

Preparation time: 25 minutes
Yield: 5 servings

Ingredients

1 tablespoon olive oil
1 cup onion , chopped
1/3 cup celery, chopped
2/3 garlic clove, minced 6cup vegetable broth
1/3 lb beef, shredded and cooked
2 cup quinoa noodles
2 cup sliced carrot
1 teaspoon dried basil
½ teaspoon dried oregano
1/3 salt and pepper

Preparation

- In a large cooking pot, add olive oil and cook celery, carrots, basil, oregano, onions and garlic in it
- Now pour in the meat pieces and vegetable broth
- Stir in the noodles and cook for about 20 minutes
- Serve and enjoy.

Sweet Potatoes And Rice Noodle Soup

For a unique combination, this soup uses sweet potatoes introduced with onions, cinnamon and coconut milk.

Yield: 4 servings
Preparation time: 20 minutes

Ingredients

1 sweet onion cut into 1-inch chunks
2 tablespoons cinnamon
1/2 teaspoon salt
2 large sweet potatoes, peeled, cubed, boiled
2 tablespoons olive oil
6 cups vegetable or chicken stock
1 cup coconut milk
1 teaspoons honey
Rice noodles (amounts as needed to serve 4 people)

Preparation

- Heat oil in a pan and add cinnamon, salt, onion and sweet potatoes
- Cook until all ingredients are combined well
- Now add chicken broth or stock and honey
- Simmer and cook for 15 minutes

- Next, add rice noodles and coconut milk
- Cook for about 5 more minutes, then serve

Cabbage And Noodle Soup

Here you go with a traditional soup recipe, prepared from some of the finest gluten-free ingredients.

Preparation time: 25 minutes
Yield: 4 servings

Ingredients

4 garlic cloves, minced
1 tablespoon tomatoes, paste form
4 cups cabbage , chopped
2 onions , diced thinly
1 cup carrot , chopped
1/3 cup green beans
1/4 cup zucchini , chopped
1/2 teaspoon oregano
2 cup rice noodles, cooked
salt & pepper, to taste
8 cups chicken broth

Preparation

- Heat oil in a non-stick pan and sauté onions in it
- Then add carrots, garlic and cook for 5 minutes
- Now add broth and tomatoes paste along with cabbage, green beans and oregano
- Sprinkle salt and pepper at the end

- Simmer this mixture for about 10 minutes and then add zucchini
- Now add the noodles and cook for about 10 more minutes
- Then serve and enjoy

Vermicelli Soup

Vermicelli soup is light soup recipe to enjoy. Made with the combination of chicken and rice noodles, this recipe hits the spot. It a great addition to our gluten-free noodle soups collection.

Preparation time: 25 minutes
Yield: 4 servings

Ingredients

10 cups water
1 cups celery, sliced
2 cup carrots, diced
4 cups chicken (cooked and cut in cubes)
200 grams rice noodles
4 cup chicken broth
½ teaspoon cumin
3 tablespoons olive oil

Preparation

- In a cooking pot, add oil and heat, and then add celery, carrots and chicken pieces
- Cook for about 5 minutes, and then add broth and water
- Let the mixture simmer
- Once the mixture comes to a boil, add the cumin and cook for about 20 minutes
- Place noodles in serving bowl and pour the soup over it.
- Enjoy.

Seafood Rice Noodle Soup

In this recipe, we are combining seafood with some mouth-watering ingredients to make a delicious dish.

Preparation time:
Yield: 4 servings

Ingredients

1 cup rice noodles, cooked
1 cup fresh mushrooms , diced
1 bok Choy, leaves separated
10 ozs shrimp
2 stalk green onions, sliced
1 cup coconut milk
4 cups vegetable broth
Salt and pepper to taste

Preparation

- In a cooking pot, add water and bring to boil
- Add the broth and simmer
- Next, add the mushrooms, Bok coy, green onions
- Sprinkle salt and pepper on top
- Now add the shrimp and cook until all the ingredients get tender and soft

- Stir in the noodles, and cook for additional 5 minutes
- Just before serving, add coconut milk and give a final stir
- Serve and enjoy.

Pumpkin And Rice Noodle Soup

A spicy and sweet soup, that can be prepared in just 15 minutes. We are combining pumpkin with coconut and rice noodles to make a creative and classic recipe this time.

Preparation time: 20 minutes
Yield: 4 servings

Ingredients

1 green onion, chopped
4 garlic cloves, crushed
2 tablespoon oil
2 tablespoons Thai red curry paste
1.5 kg pumpkin
600 ml chicken stock
200 g rice noodles
3500 ml coconut milk

Preparation

- Cook pumpkin in chicken stock until tender
- In a cooking pan add oil and sauté onions and add garlic, curry powder transfer this mixture to pumpkin pan
- Next, puree with blender once cooled
- Next, add the noodles and cook for more 5 minute
- Serve hot and enjoy

Appetizer Recipes

Coconut Noodle Soup

Soup can be a conversation starter as an appetizer at the start of a meal. This recipe is a perfect blend of texture, color and flavors. Coconut adds a versatile flavor and great texture to the recipe.

Preparation time: 10 minutes
Yield: 4 servings

Ingredients

2 tablespoons red curry paste
350 grams coconut milk
200 grams mushrooms, chopped
1 package wide rice noodles, cooked according to package instructions
1 green chili, sliced in the shape of rings
1 bunch spring onions, diced

Preparation

- In a cooking pot, add curry powder and cook for one minute
- Add in the coconut milk and half cup of water.

- Cook until simmer and then add mushrooms, chili and spring onion
- Cook for about 18 minutes and at the end mix in the noodles.
- Cook for one minute then serve

Mini Ham, Chesses And Noodles Cups

Preparation time: 20 minutes
Yield: 4 servings

Ingredients

4 cups quinoa noodles, cooked
4 egg whites
1 cup ham, cooked and shredded
1 cup chicken, cooked and shredded
1 cup shredded sharp cheddar cheese
1/4 cup parsley (chopped)
2 tablespoons cottage cheese
2 tomatoes, thinly diced
Salt and pepper to taste
1 cup cooked quinoa

Preparation

- Combine all the listed ingredients in bowl
- Line the paper muffins in a muffin tray and then pour the mixture into each muffin cup

- Heat oven at 375 degree F
- Bake the muffins in the oven for about 25 minutes
- Once done serve and enjoy

Vegetables And Quinoa Noodle Bites

A recipe that combines vegetables in a mouth-watering way. If you are not a fan of vegetables, then this recipe is a good way to "fool" yourself into eating your daily veggies.

Preparation time: 20 minutes
Yield: 6 servings

Ingredients

1 cup quinoa, cooked
2 organic eggs, beaten
1 green onion stalk, diced
1 cup parmesan cheese, shredded
4 tablespoons cilantro, chopped
3 tablespoons of flour
Salt and pepper to taste
3 tablespoons lime juice

Preparation

- Preheat oven at 375 degree F.
- Mix all the listed ingredients in a bowl.
- Grease the mini muffin pan with oil and scoop the mixture in to the muffin spots,
- Bake in oven at 375 degree F, for 20 minutes.

- Once brown and crisp, serve and enjoy.

Rice Noodles Salad

A delicious salad in with you can combine any type of vegetables, you liked. A recipe full of nutrition and healthy ingredients.

Preparation time: 10 minutes
Yield: 4 servings

Ingredients
1 cup of quinoa, cooked
1 onion, chopped
1 cloves garlic, minced
4 celery sticks, diced
4 carrots, peeled and chopped
½ tablespoon cumin
1 bunch of baby kale, finely chopped
4 tomatoes, diced
1 cucumber, diced
2 avocado, peeled, pitted and diced
4 tablespoons of lemon juice

For the dressing
6 tablespoons olive oil
Sea salt and freshly ground black
5 tablespoons of lime juice

Preparation

- Combine all the listed ingredients in the bowl and toss well to coat well
- Once done, serve and enjoy.

Vegetable Noodle Soup

Another old standard soup recipe to enjoy at lunch or dinner as an appetizer.

Preparation time: 15 minutes
Yield: 5 servings

Ingredients

1 cup carrots, cubed
1 cup cucumber, cubed
½ cup kale, chopped
2 cup corn kernels, boiled
1 cup rice noodles, boiled and half broken
1 garlic clove
Sal and pepper to taste
½ tablespoons cumin
5 tablespoons olive oil
5 cups chicken stock

Preparation

- In a cooking pot, heat oil and sauté the onions.
- Add garlic and cook for one more minute
- Then add carrots, kale, cucumber, corn kernel and cook for more 5 minutes
- Now add stock along with seasonings.
- Cook for 15 minutes. Once the all ingredients cooked properly, add in noodles and then stir twice.
- Serve and enjoy.

Quinoa Noodle Appetizer Time Soup

It is a light and delicious soup recipe to enjoy as an appetizer.

Preparation time: 20 minutes
Yield: 4 servings

Ingredients

1 cup cooked quinoa
1 cup cooked quinoa noodles
3 chicken breasts
10 cups chicken stock
6 large carrots, sliced
1 cup corn kernels, boiled
2 teaspoons parsley
2 teaspoons garlic

Salt and pepper
1 bay leaf
1 green onion, chopped

Preparation

- Place all the listed ingredients (excluding noodles) in the pot and cook on low heat for about 25 minutes
- Now add noodles and cook for additional 10 minutes
- One done, serve and enjoy

Avocado And Rice Noodle Salads

A unique salad that combines the popular flavors of avocados and pineapple. Ready in just 5 minutes.

Preparation time: 5 minutes
Yield: 2 servings

Ingredients

1 tablespoons lime juice
1 cup avocados, sliced
1 cup pineapples, sliced
1 cup rice (or quinoa) noodles, boiled
Salt and pepper to taste
Pinch of sugar

Preparation

- Combine all the listed ingredients in the bowl and toss well to combine all the ingredients
- Once done, serve and enjoy.

Black Beans With Rice Noodles Appetizer

A great appetizer that is full of fiber, mineral and protein.

Preparation time: 5 minutes
Yield: 4 servings

Ingredients

1 cup black beans, boiled and drained
2 cups rice noodles
1 cup cucumber, cubed
1 cup cherry tomatoes
4 tablespoons lime juice
Salt and pepper to taste

Preparation

- Combine all the listed ingredients in a bowl and toss well for flavorful combination
- Serve and enjoy.

Eggplant And Rice Noodles

Here we are with a combination of fried eggplant and rice noodles. The smooth eggplant goes well with creamy texture of the noodles. The recipe is made in just 15 minutes and tastes just perfect.

Preparation time: 10 minutes
Yield: 4 servings

Ingredients

2 large eggplants, cut in cubes
1 tablespoon lime juice
Salt and pepper to taste
2 cups rice noodles
1 tablespoon nutmeg, powder
Olive oil for frying, about 2 cups
Cottage cheese for texture

Preparation

- Fry the eggplant in olive oil and set aside.
- In a bowl, combine noodles with salt, pepper, lime juice and nutmeg
- Add in the cottage cheese and fried eggplant
- Serve and enjoy this light appetizer

Meal Plans For 3 Weeks

What can you eat as a gluten-challenged person? To help you get started, here are 3 weeks of basic meal plans based on this collection of recipes. Mix and match as you prefer.

WEEK 1

Breakfast: 2 fruit based and one egg based meals, 1 smoothie drink

Rice Noodles with Eggs and Potatoes
Fruity Bites
Fruity French Toast Casserole
Kiwi Smoothie

Lunch: 2 vegetables, 3 meat or fish based meals, 2 appetizers

Prawns with Quinoa Noodles
Quinoa Noodles with Chili
Peanut and Sesame Rice Noodles
Beef, Broccoli and Rice Noodles Stir Fry
Chicken, Vegetables and Rice Stir Fry
Black Beans with Rice Noodle Appetizer
Rice noodle salad

Dinner: 1 beef, 2 chicken, 4 soup, 2 vegetable

Beef, Eggs and Rice Noodles
Vegetable Noodles Stir-Fry
Sesame Chicken
Battered Chicken Fry with Rice Noodles and Sweet and Sour Sauce
Quinoa Noodles with Spinach and Tomatoes
Vermicelli Soup
Seafood Rice Noodle Soup
Cabbage and Noodle Soup
Potatoes and Rice Noodle Soup

WEEK 2

Breakfast: 1 vegetable based, 2 noodles, 3 fruit based, 1 drink

Gluten-Free Quinoa Noodles Recipe
Rice Noodles with Eggs and Potatoes
Fruity Bites
Fruity French toast Casserole
Banana Waffles
Purple Pineapple Drink
Kiwi smoothie

Lunch: 1 vegetable based recipe, 2 soups, 1 chicken, 1 sea food recipe, 1 beef, 1 drink

Chicken, Vegetables and Rice Stir Fry
Prawn with Quinoa Noodles
Quinoa Noodles with Chiles

Beef, Broccoli and Rice Noodles Stir Fry
Pumpkin and Rice Noodle Soup
Seafood Rice Noodle Soup
Purple Pineapple Drink

Dinner: 2 meat, 2 chicken, 1 vegetable 3 Appetizers soups, 1 salad

Eggplant and Rice Noodles
Black Beans with Rice Noodles Appetizer
Quinoa Noodles Appetizer Time Soup
Avocadoes and Rice Noodle Salads
Vegetable Noodles Stir-Fry
Sesame Chicken
Chicken Delight
Beef, Eggs and Rice Noodles
Pork Stir Fry with Rice Noodles

WEEK 3

Breakfast: 1 drink, 1 egg recipe, 3 fruit, 1 noodle

Purple pineapple drink
Rice Noodles with Eggs and Potatoes
Gluten Free Quinoa Noodles Recipe
Banana Waffles
Fruity French Toast Casserole
Fruity Bites

Lunch: 2 appetizers, 2 soups, 3 snacks, 1 vegetable, 1 chicken, 1 meat

Chicken, Vegetables and Rice Stir Fry
Prawns with Quinoa Noodles
Quinoa Noodles with Chiles
Beef, Broccoli and Rice Noodles Stir Fry
Mini Ham, Chesses and Noodles Cups
Easy Noodles Soup Recipe
Rice Noodles Soup with lemon Chicken
Yogurt Popsicle
Dry Fruit Rolls
Coconut Noodles Soup

Dinner: 3 meat based mix, 2 snacks, 3 soups

Chicken Delight
Beef, Eggs and Rice Noodles
Pork Stir Fry with Rice Noodles
Mango Pudding
Stuffed Mushrooms
Thai Style Noodle Soup
Rice Noodles Soup with lemon Chicken
Rice Noodle Soup with Chicken

Gluten Free Shopping List

This list covers ingredients used in the recipes found in this book.

Fruits

Bananas

Blueberries

Apples

Kiwi

Mangos

Apricots

Cherries

Pineapple

Vegetables

Onions

Zucchini

Red bell peppers

White potatoes

Mushrooms

Garlic

Green onions

Snow peas

Carrots

Spring onion

Lemon

Ginger

Broccoli

Tomatoes

Lime

Chinese chiles

Baby spinach

Cherry tomatoes

Cilantro

Sweet potatoes

Capsicum

Lemongrass

Broccolini

Choy sum

Spring mint

Jalapeno

Mint leaves

Celery

Black olives

Basil

Tomatoes

Cabbage

Green beans

Bok choy

Pumpkin

Baby kale

Avocado

Cucumber

Cherry tomatoes

Eggplants

Meat/Poultry/Seafood

Eggs

Chicken

Beef

Prawns

Parmesan cheese

Pork tenderloins

Dairy cream

Yogurt

Cottage cheese

Grains (Gluten-Free)

Rice noodles

Quinoa noodles

Quinoa flakes

Rice flour

Gluten free bread (paleo bread)

Quinoa

Jasmine rice

Corn flour

Corn kernels

Beans/Seeds/Nuts

Dates

Walnuts

Nutmeg

Almonds

Peanuts

Tofu

Pinto beans

Black beans

Sesame seeds

Alternative Milks

Rice milk

Coconut milk

Soy milk

Almond milk

Oils

Olive oil

Almond oil

Sunflower oil

Sesame oil

Peanut oil

Sweeteners/Flavoring

Honey

Agave nectar

Vanilla extract

Part 2

Introduction

Not many people are aware of the different types of noodles you can cook at home. There are virtually dozens of different varieties of noodles available. If you love cooking and eating noodles, it is a good idea for you to learn some basics about the various types of noodles you can try and enjoy.

You will find pertinent information about each noodle type as well as what it is made of. Moreover, you will get to learn a number of recipes you can make with the three types of noodles covered in this cookbook. You can choose the recipes that appeal to you the most and make them at home. We have tried our best to make the recipes as simple to follow as possible.

To make the most of the information provided in this cookbook, you have to read it from cover to cover. We will start off with Udon noodles, their history and the recipes you can make using them. Happy reading!

Types Of Noodles & The Recipes

As mentioned above, we are going to cover a few types of noodles as well as their recipes. Without further ado, we will get started with Udon noodles.

Udon Noodles

Udon noodles originate from traditional Japanese cuisine. They are made of thick wheat flour. Usually served as noodle soup, Udon noodles can be used in a wide range of recipes. They are topped with prawn and tempura but you can use any ingredients you want.

The story behind Udon noodles is that they have been around since flour milling began in Japan. That was way back in the 13th century, which means that Udon noodles have been eaten for almost 8 centuries now. However, there are different accounts of how they came about. It is difficult to pinpoint the exact origin.

Udon noodles are widely available in the US. You can even purchase them as instant noodles. They are available in both dried and frozen form. It is up to you to decide which one you prefer. Buy the noodles and use them to make one of the recipes that follow. Let's look at the top recipes that use Udon noodles:

To start things off, here is one of the most popular Udon noodles recipes:

Ingredients
- ¾ teaspoon Five Spice Powder
- 2 tablespoons Almond Oil
- 8 ounces sliced Crimini Mushrooms
- Salt, to taste
- ½ teaspoon Cayenne Powder
- ½lb sliced fresh Asparagus
- 1/3 cup Soy Sauce
- 5 cups Water
- ¼ cup Honey
- 8 ounces dried Udon Noodles
- 2 finely chopped Garlic Cloves

Instructions

☐ Combine the soy sauce, honey, salt, five spice powder and cayenne pepper in a bowl. Whisk them together until smooth.

☐ Boil the Udon noodles till they are cooked perfectly. Follow the instructions given on the package to get the best texture. Drizzle some oil on top of the cooked noodles to keep them separated.

☐ Pour the 5 cups of water into a large saucepan. Bring to a boil and add the asparagus. Blanche the asparagus slices for a minute or so. Then remove them and place in a bowl.

☐Take a large skillet, pour the olive oil in it and heat it over medium-high heat. In the oil, cook the garlic until it turns golden brown.
☐Add mushrooms to the garlic and stir-fry for up to 2 minutes. Sprinkle a pinch of salt and five spice powder over the mushrooms while cooking.
☐Mix in the asparagus and cook for 3 minutes. Check if the asparagus is tender. If not, keep cooking.
☐Pour in the sauce you made in the first step. Add the noodles as well and mix well together.

Your five spice mushrooms with Udon noodles is ready. Eat it immediately to get the best flavor!

Udon Noodle Miso Soup

Ingredients

- 12 ounces Udon Noodles
- 2 tablespoons White Miso
- 4 cups Chicken Stock (substitute with Vegetable Stock if you want)
- ½ cup fresh Mushrooms
- ½ cup sliced Carrots
- ½ cup Green Onions
- ½ cup Snow Peas sliced diagonally

Instructions

☐ Boil the udon noodles following the directions provided on the package. Drain the water and then set the noodles aside.

☐ Take a large saucepan and bring the stock to a boil over medium-high heat. Decrease the heat to medium and then add carrots. Keep cooking till the carrots have a crispy and tender feel. This should take around 2 minutes.

☐ Add in the snow peas and cook for a further minute or so until the peas are tender but still green.

☐ Put in the mushrooms and cook for 30 more seconds. Turn the heat off and remove the saucepan from the stove.

☐ In a medium-sized bowl, combine the miso and 1 ladleful of the broth mixture. Whisk till the miso is dissolved in the broth. Transfer the contents to the saucepan and mix slightly.

☐ Add the green onions and cooked noodles to the saucepan and stir till they mix perfectly.

The tasty and highly nutritious Udon Noodle Miso Soup is ready!

Peanut Udon Noodles

Ingredients

- 8 ounces dry Udon Noodles

- 4 tablespoons Water
- 2 tablespoons Soy Sauce
- ½ cup Natural Peanut Butter
- ¼ cup chopped & roasted Peanuts
- 2 tablespoons Rice Vinegar
- 4 ounces Snow Peas (Remove the strings beforehand)
- 1 minced Garlic Clove
- 1 tablespoon toasted Sesame Oil
- Red Pepper Flakes, to taste
- 1 teaspoon grated fresh Ginger
- 2 teaspoons Brown Sugar

Instructions

☐ Read the instructions on the noodles packet and cook according to them. Around a minute before the noodles are fully cooked, add the snow peas. Drain the water and set the noodles aside.

☐ In a large bowl, whisk together the peanut butter, red pepper flakes, ginger, garlic, rice vinegar, sesame oil and soy sauce. To get the desired texture, add one tablespoon of water at a time. You have to make the mixture smooth but not bland.

☐ Transfer the peanut sauce to the pot/dish in which you cooked the noodles. Toss and mix to get the sauce spread out evenly.

Sprinkle the roasted almonds on top and enjoy your Peanut Udon Noodles.

Thai Chicken Udon Soup

Ingredients

- 6 ounces dry Udon Noodles
- ¼ teaspoon Kosher Salt
- 3 crushed Garlic Cloves
- 1 minced Garlic Clove
- 1 tablespoon Honey
- 1 tablespoon Almond Oil
- 1 star Anise
- ¼ cup Green Onions (Cut diagonally)
- 1 Green Onion (2-inch pieces)
- 2 teaspoons peeled & minced fresh Ginger
- 6 slices peeled fresh Ginger
- 4 cups Chicken Stock
- 8 ounces shredded Chicken Breast
- 1 tablespoon Soy Sauce
- 3 ½ ounces Shiitake Mushrooms
- ¼ cup Sake

Instructions

☐ Slice the mushrooms thinly, removing the stems before you start. In a saucepan, combine the chicken stock, anise, 2-inch green onion pieces, ginger slices and the mushroom stems and bring to a boil over medium-high heat.

☐ Once boiled, cover the saucepan, lower the heat and let the mixture simmer for a further 20 minutes. Take the saucepan off the stove and let it sit for around 10 minutes.

☐ Next, drain the stock and throw out any solids that remain.

☐ Boil the udon noodles following the instructions provided on the packet. Drain the noodles and then rinse with cool water before keeping them aside.

☐ Pour the oil in the saucepan and heat over medium-high heat. Toss in the mushrooms and sauté them for 2 minutes. Add in the minced garlic and ginger and sauté for 1 more minute.

☐ Add the sake to the saucepan and cook for 4 minutes. Scrape the pan to remove any bits stuck on the bottom.

☐ Take the stock and pour it into the saucepan. Bring the mixture to a boil and reduce the heat, bringing it down to medium-low. Add the remaining ingredients except the noodles and the green onions and cook till the chicken is properly done.

☐ Combine with the noodles and sprinkle green onions on top.

You will surely love the Thai Chicken Udon Soup.

Spicy Udon Noodle Bowl

Ingredients

- 2 packets Udon Noodles
- 2 tablespoons Almond Oil
- 1 tablespoon minced Garlic
- 2 thinly sliced Filament Sticks
- 1 tablespoon minced Ginger
- 3 tablespoons Chili Paste
- 3 cups Chicken Broth
- 1 ½ tablespoons Lime Juice
- 1 thinly sliced Onion
- 2 tablespoons sliced Mustard Tubers
- 5 dried & thinly sliced Shiitake Mushrooms
- Salt, to taste
- 1 tablespoon Extra Virgin Olive Oil

Instructions

☐ Follow the instructions on the packet to cook the Udon noodles. However, don't add any salt or oil to the noodles when boiling them. Drain the noodles before setting them aside.

☐ In a large saucepan, pour in the oils. Sauté the onion, garlic and ginger in the oil for a couple of minutes. Toss in the mushrooms and keep cooking till the onions are completely soft.

☐ Add the remaining ingredients, except the noodles, to the mixture and simmer it for up to 10 minutes.

☐ Lay out the noodles in a serving dish and pour the Spicy Udon Soup over it.

The Spicy Udon Noodle Bowl may be a little 'hot' for some but is totally worth trying.

Yaki Udon

Ingredients

- 1 teaspoon Mirin
- 2 ounces shredded Cabbage
- 1 chopped Scallion
- ½ thinly sliced Onion
- 2 tablespoons Soy Sauce
- 2 tablespoons Almond Oil
- ½ large Carrot (Cut into matchsticks)
- 6 ounces thinly sliced Pork
- 12 ounces frozen Udon Noodles
- 1 teaspoon Worcestershire Sauce

Instructions

☐ Cook the noodles according to the instructions on the packet. Drain and transfer to a colander. Leave it in the colander for some time so they drain properly.

☐ Take a small bowl and pour in the Worcestershire sauce, soy sauce and Mirin.

☐Bring the almond oil to heat in a wok and stir-fry the onion until it is completely soft. Add the pork and keep cooking till the pork changes color. Toss in the cabbage and carrot and stir-fry till the cabbage goes soft. This shouldn't take more than 2 minutes.
☐To the wok, add the noodles and continue to stir-fry for 1 more minute. Toss the noodles so they mix perfectly with the sauce. Add the scallion, stir once and then turn the heat off.

To add an extra zing to your Yaki Udon, you can sprinkle Bonito flakes on top before tucking in.

Lemongrass Chicken Udon

Ingredients

- 1 handful chopped Cilantro
- 1/3 cup Rice Wine Vinegar
- 4 sliced Chicken Breasts
- 1 ½ teaspoons Cornstarch
- 2 tablespoons Almond Oil
- ¼ cup Soy Sauce
- 1 tablespoon Brown Sugar
- 1 chopped and processed Lemongrass stalk
- ½ cup Chicken Broth
- 8 ounces Udon Noodles
- 1 finely chopped Shallot
- Red Pepper Flakes, to taste
- 2 tablespoons grated fresh Ginger
- Vegetables (sliced Bok Choy, thinly sliced Mushrooms, julienned Carrots, diagonally sliced Scallions & 1/2-inch Broccoli slices), any quantity you want. Decide according to quantity of noodles.

Instructions

☐ Combine the red pepper flakes, cilantro, rice wine vinegar, shallot, brown sugar, lemongrass, soy sauce and ginger in a bowl. Take a third of the mixture and apply it to the chicken.

☐ In a large pot, bring water to a boil and cook the carrots and broccoli for up to 3 minutes. Remove the vegetables from the water.

☐ Cook the noodles in the used water following the instructions on the packet. Once boiled, drain the noodles.

☐ Stir-fry the chicken in a skillet over medium-high heat in the almond oil. Make sure the chicken is fully cooked. If it is, add the mushrooms and cook for a couple of minutes.

☐ Throw in the scallions and bok choy and cook for 2 more minutes. The bok choy should start wilting at this point.

☐ Add the carrots and broccoli to the mixture and stir well. Add the remaining 2/3 of the marinade to the mixture and keep stirring.

☐ In a large bowl, pour in the chicken broth and mix the cornstarch in.

☐ Combine the chicken, mixtures and noodles. Toss well to get the blend perfect.

You can enhance the flavor of your Lemongrass Chicken Udon by topping it with cilantro or even chopped cashews.

Meaty Kishimen Noodles

Ingredients
- 8 ounces frozen Udon Noodles
- 2 slices half-strip Bacon
- ½ teaspoon ground Garlic
- 5 grams Butter
- ¼ sliced Onion
- 1 slice sliced Cheese
- 1 Egg Yolk
- 100ml Almond Milk
- Salt & Pepper, to taste
- Dash of Parsley

Instructions

☐ Put the frozen udon noodles in the microwave at 600W for 3 minutes.

☐ Place a frying pan over medium heat and melt the butter. Fry the garlic in the butter and then add onion and bacon. When cooked properly, add the cheese and milk and bring the mixture to a boil.

☐ Combine the mixture with the noodles and toss. Season the noodles with salt and pepper. Add egg yolks, beating them beforehand.

Sprinkle the parsley on top and enjoy.

Udon With Grated Daikon & Beef

Ingredients
- 1 tablespoon Sake
- 6 ounces Udon Noodles
- 2 tablespoons Soy Sauce
- 50ml Water
- 2 tablespoons Hon-Mirin
- ½ tablespoon Sugar
- 200g thinly sliced Beef
- Grated Daikon Radish, as much as desired
- 100ml Mentsuyu Sauce

Instructions
☐ Heat up the Mentsuyu to dilute it. Keep in mind that it has to be added to the broth.

☐ Take a pot and combine the soy sauce, water, sugar, hon-mirin and sake. Add the beef to the ingredients and break it while cooking. Make sure the beef is well cooked and then turn off the heat. Let the pot stand for 30 minutes as is.

☐ Prepare the udon noodles according to the instructions provided on the packet. Drain and rinse with cool water.
☐ Layer the mixture and noodles in a serving bowl and top it off with the remaining ingredients.

Eat hot to get the best flavor.

Carbonara Udon Noodles

Ingredients
- 6 slices thinly sliced Pork Belly
- 1 grated Garlic Clove
- 600ml Mentsuyu Sauce
- 2 packets boiled Udon Noodles
- 1 diagonally sliced Japanese Leek

Instructions
☐ Dilute the sauce with water and boil the mixture. Add the remaining ingredients except the Udon noodles. Cook until the leek softens up.

☐ Mix the noodles with the mixture and simmer for a few minutes.

Remove from heat and eat right away.

Stir Fried Udon Noodles With Nori Seaweed Paste

Ingredients

- 2 packets cooked Udon Noodles
- ¼ sliced Onion
- 50g Shrimp
- 2 leaves Cabbage
- 3 tablespoons Nori Seaweed Paste
- 1 thinly sliced Carrot
- 1 teaspoon Almond Oil

Instructions
☐ Chop the cabbage into small pieces. Combine with other vegetables in a small bowl and cover the bowl with plastic wrap. Put in the microwave for 1 minute.
☐Remove the vegetables from the bowl and put in the noodles. Microwave for a minute.

☐Heat the oil in a frying pan and stir fry the vegetables and shrimp.

☐Once the ingredients are properly cooked, combine with noodles. Also pour some water into the frying pan.

☐Cook the noodles until little water is left in the frying pan, and then pour in the nori seaweed paste. Taste and add more if needed.

☐When the paste is mixed into the dish, remove the pan from heat and serve.

Udon Noodles With Chilled Tomatoes

Ingredients

- 2 packets cooked Udon Noodles
- 2 Tomatoes
- ½ Cucumber
- ½ Onion
- A pinch of White Sesame Seeds
- 100 ml Citrus Flavored Vinegar Sauce
- 1 tablespoon Sesame Oil
- A pinch of Black Pepper

Instructions

☐ Chop the tomatoes and cucumber into small cubes, and finely slice the onion.

☐ Transfer the vegetables to a bowl and add black pepper, vinegar sauce and sesame oil. Place the bowl in the fridge overnight.

☐ Cook the noodles as per package instructions. Then drain the water from the noodles and run under cold water.

☐Pour the noodles onto a dish and ladle the vegetable mixture from the night before.
☐Garnish the noodles with sesame seeds and they're ready to eat!

Creamy Curry Udon

Ingredients

- 3 packets Frozen Udon Noodles
- 100 g Readymade Curry Roux Block
- 150 g Pork
- 2 teaspoons Potato Starch Flour
- 750 ml Water
- Oil, as required
- 3 tablespoons Fresh Cream
- ½ Onion
- 150 ml Milk
- 1 Scallion

Instructions
☐ Cut the pork into bite-size pieces, and slice the onion thinly.
☐ Placing a little oil in a frying pan, fry both the things until they are cooked well.
☐ When cooked, add milk and water to the frying pan.
☐ When the mixture begins to bubble, dissolve the curry roux followed by the fresh cream.
☐ Turn the heat down a notch. Dissolve the potato starch in 2 tablespoons of water separately and add this to the pan, stirring well.
☐ Prepare the udon noodles in a separate pan. When ready, pour these into serving bowl and pour the prepared mixture over it.

Garnish your dish with chopped scallions and a little fresh cream.

So, we have covered a number of udon recipes for you to try at home. Once you get the hang of cooking the noodles, for which the instructions are provided, you shouldn't face any problems cooking udon noodles and the recipes based on them.

Ramen Noodles
Ramen noodles originate from China and are considered to be among the more popular types of Asian noodles in the world today. According to estimates, nearly 95 billion Ramen-based meals were consumed across the globe in 2011. Ramen noodles

have become a convenient food to make at home and students on limited budgets eat ramen noodles as an inexpensive alternative.

The noodles are made from wheat. You can find a number of different types of ramen noodles available on the market but not all of them are of equal quality. Therefore, it is important for you to select the best type of ramen noodles based on the recipe you are making.

Traditionally, ramen noodles are used in soup-based dishes in Japan. In fact, the term 'Ramen' means a Japanese boiled noodle dish. The soups are then topped off with different ingredients to enhance the flavor. In this cookbook, we will look at a number of different Ramen noodle recipes, not necessarily ones based on soups.

Chili Chicken Ramen Noodles

Ingredients

- 8 ounces Ramen Noodles
- 1 tablespoon Extra Virgin Olive Oil
- 3 teaspoons Sugar
- 2 tablespoons Hot Chili Sauce
- 1 thinly sliced Red Onion
- 2 teaspoons Soy Sauce
- 2 liters fresh Chicken Stock
- 2 teaspoon Almond Oil
- 3 tablespoons Korean Chili Paste
- 1 teaspoon Fish Sauce
- 2 boneless and skinless Chicken Legs

Instructions

☐ Combine the chicken with the almond oil, 2 tablespoons Korean chili paste, 2 teaspoons sugar and soy sauce. Rub in the ingredients properly and leave the chicken aside for 2 hours.

☐ For the Ramen sauce, take a small bowl and mix the hot chili sauce, 1 teaspoon sugar, 1 tablespoon Korean chili paste and fish sauce.
☐ Bring the chicken stock to a boil in a large saucepan.
☐ Grill the marinated chicken and cook it properly.
☐ Cook the noodles following the instructions on the packet.
☐ Combine the Ramen sauce, noodles and chicken and eat right away.

It might be a bit spicy for some but you will love it!

Chicken Fajita Ramen Noodles

Ingredients

- 1 packet Ramen Noodles (cook and drain)
- 2 sliced Green Peppers
- Salt and Red Pepper Flakes, to taste
- 1 sliced Onion
- 1lb cubed Chicken Breast
- 2 sliced Red Peppers
- 1 packet Taco Seasoning
- 1 can stewed Tomatoes
- 1lb bulk Italian Sausage

Instructions

☐ In a large pot, cook the sausages till they are brown. Cut the sausages into small pieces.

☐ Toss the chicken into the pot and sauté with the sausages.

☐ Add the seasonings, including tomatoes, Taco seasoning, salt and red pepper along with the onions to the chicken and sausages. Cook the mixture till the onions are soft.

☐ Next add the peppers and cook the mixtures till they are soft to touch.

☐ Lay out the noodles in a serving dish and top it off with the fajita sauce.

Eat hot to enjoy the flavor!

Cheesy Ramen Meat Pie

Ingredients

- ¼ cup diced Jalapeno Peppers
- 2 packets Beef Ramen Noodles
- 1 tablespoon Chili Powder
- 1 can Hormel Chili
- 8 sliced-thin Velveeta Cheese
- ¼ bag Nacho Doritos
- Disposable Pie Pan

Instructions
☐ Boil 3 cups of water in a large saucepan. Add the noodles and cook them for around 5 minutes. Stir them once to ensure they don't stick together. Drain and set the noodles aside.
☐ In a saucepan, heat up the Hormel Chili.
☐ Butter the pie pan you bought.
☐ Crush the Doritos and sprinkle them at the bottom of the pan. Make sure the base is completely covered. On top of the Doritos add 1/4th of the noodles followed by 1/4th of the sauce and then cheese. Keep layering and

repeat the pattern till you have added all the ingredients. The Doritos should be on top when you finish.

☐Set your oven to 350o and bake for 15 minutes. Keep checking to ensure the mixture is fully cooked.

Tuck in to the cheesy treat you have made!

Italian Ramen Pizza Pie

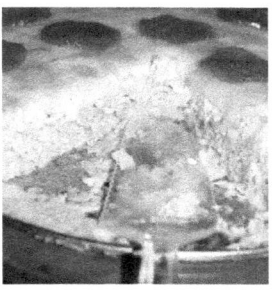

Ingredients

- 2 packets Ramen Noodles
- ½ cup Tomato Sauce
- ¼ shredded Asiago Cheese
- 2 tablespoons Parmesan Cheese
- 10 pieces Pepperoni
- 1 tablespoon Italian Seasoning Blend
- 1 cup shredded Mozzarella Cheese

Instructions

☐ Cook the ramen noodles according to the instructions provided on the packet. Drain the noodles and transfer to a large bowl. Combine with the seasoning blend and Parmesan cheese.

☐ Mold the mixture into the shape of a pizza pie.

☐ Grease a large skillet and heat it up. Place the pie in the skillet and cook for around 3 minutes. The noodles should be crunchy by this time. Then, flip the pie over and cook for a further 3 minutes.

☐ Set your oven to 375oF. Put the pie in the oven, topping it off with the cheeses, pepperoni and tomato sauce. Cook for around 5 minutes or until the cheese melts completely.

Don't let the pizza pie get cold and eat right away.

Pineapple Meatballs Ramen

Ingredients

- 2 packets Ramen Noodles
- ½ pound ground Beef
- 1/3 cup Vegetable Oil
- 3 tablespoons Worcestershire Sauce
- 4 cups Water
- 2 teaspoons Garlic Powder
- ½ cup sliced Pineapples
- 1 teaspoon Salt
- ½ cup sliced Red Peppers

Instructions

☐ Boil water in a pot and add the noodle cakes to it.

☐ Let the noodles cook for 4-5 minutes or until they are separated.

☐ Drain all water from the noodles and run them under cold water.

☐ In a large bowl, combine the Worcestershire sauce, salt and garlic powder, and add the ground beef to it. Coat the beef with the ingredients.
☐ Make medium sized meatballs from the beef.
☐ Cook the meatballs in vegetable oil in a frying pan until they are well browned. Reduce heat and cook for another 10 minutes.
☐ Before the meatballs are fully cooked, add red peppers and pineapples to the frying pan. Fry for 5 minutes, remove from heat and transfer everything to a plate.

Enjoy to your satisfaction!

Teriyaki Chow Mein

Ingredients

- 1 packet Beef flavored Maruchan Ramen
- 4 ounces Flank Steak, cut into ¼ inch slices
- ¼ cup Teriyaki Sauce
- 14 ounces Beef Broth
- 4 ounces sliced Mushrooms
- 2 medium sized sliced Green Onions
- ½ teaspoon Celery Salt
- ½ sliced Celery Stalk
- 2 minced Garlic Cloves
- 1½ tablespoons Cornstarch
- ½ cup finely chopped Broccoli

Instructions

☐ Set a medium sized wok to medium high heat and pour in teriyaki sauce and beef broth.

☐ Next, add mushrooms, celery, celery salt, garlic, broccoli and green onions to the wok.

☐ Boil the ingredients and then reduce the heat and let simmer for 10 minutes.

☐ Sauté the flank steak in a skillet until it loses its pink color.

☐ When the mixture in the wok is cooked well, and the steak is cooked, transfer the steak to the wok with the ramen noodles and cook for 3 minutes.

☐ Mix cornstarch in a little water, and add this to the wok. Remove the mixture from heat, only to return it after 3-5 minutes.

☐This time, lower the heat and let the mixture simmer for 5 minutes, or until the broth is thick.

Transfer the delicacy to a serving bowl and eat it immediately.

Vegetable Ramen Soup

Ingredients

- 6 ounces Ramen Noodles
- 4 cups Chicken Broth
- 15 ounces diced Tomatoes
- 1 medium sized diced Onion
- 4 Green Onions
- 1 diced Zucchini
- 2 diced Carrots
- A handful of chopped Cilantro
- 2 diced Celery Stalks
- 1 cup Water
- Juice of 1 Lime
- 1 tablespoon Olive Oil
- Sriracha Sauce, to taste

- Salt, as required
- Pepper, as required

Instructions

☐ Heat olive oil in a pot over medium heat.

☐ When heated, add zucchini, carrots, onion and celery, and sauté the vegetables for 6 minutes, or until softened.

☐ Sprinkle salt and pepper on the vegetables, followed by tomatoes, broth, lime juice and water. Let the mixture boil.

☐ When boiled, add ramen noodles and reduce the heat, cooking until the noodles are tender.

☐ Transfer the noodles to a serving bowl and top with Sriracha sauce, cilantro and green onions.

Waste no time in savoring the unique flavor of this noodle recipe.

Ramen Pudding

Ingredients

- 9 ounces Ramen Noodles
- 2 thinly sliced Bananas
- 2 large Eggs
- ½ cup Golden Raisins
- ¼ cup shredded Coconut
- 14 ounces Coconut Milk
- 4 tablespoons melted Unsalted Butter
- ½ cup Sour Cream
- 2 tablespoons Sliced Almonds
- 1½ tablespoons Almond Extract
- ¼ cup chopped Crystallized Ginger
- ¼ cup crushed Anise Seed
- ¼ teaspoon ground Cardamom
- 2/3 cup Sugar
- Salt, as required

Instructions
☐Preheat your oven to 350F, and lubricate the base of an 8 by 8 baking dish.

☐ Cover the base of the dish with sliced bananas.
☐ Place 3 noodle cakes in a bowl and pour steaming water on top. Let the noodles separate from one another, and then drain all the water.
☐ Mix melted butter with the noodles and toss to mix properly.
☐ Combine eggs, coconut milk, sour cream, cardamom, almond extract, anise seed, sugar and a pinch of salt in a large bowl and blend well.
☐ Add noodles, ginger and raisins to the bowl and mix thoroughly.
☐ Pour the mixture in the baking dish, and top with coconut and sliced almonds.
☐ Place the dish in the preheated oven and bake for 1 hour, or until golden brown.
☐ When the time is up, remove the dish from the oven and let cool for 1 hour.

Slice the pudding and serve cooled.

Ramen Noodle Salad

Ingredients

- 1 packet raw & crushed Ramen Noodles
- 8 ounces Cole Slaw
- ½ cup Oil
- ¼ cup Sugar
- ¼ cup Sunflower Seeds
- ¼ cup Cider Vinegar

Instructions

☐In a large bowl, mix together the noodles, Cole slaw and sunflower seeds.

☐In a separate bowl, pour the seasoning that comes with the noodle packet, and mix it with oil, vinegar and sugar.

☐Incorporate the two mixtures and stir well.

☐Refrigerate the final mixture for at least 2 hours.

After the allotted time has elapsed, heat and serve.

Ramen Pad Thai

Ingredients

- 4 ounces Shrimp Ramen Noodles
- 6 medium sized Shrimp
- 1 lightly beaten Egg
- 2 thinly sliced Scallions
- ¼ cup Bean Sprouts
- 1 teaspoon Fish Sauce
- Juice of 1 Lime
- 2 tablespoons crushed Peanuts

Instructions

☐ Remove the shells from the shrimps and devein them.

☐ Place the noodles in boiling water and boil them until they begin to part from each other.

☐ Add shrimp to the boiled noodles and cook for two minutes.

☐ Turn off the heat and pour the beaten egg into the noodles.

☐ Drain the water from the pan and transfer the dish to a bowl.

☐ Add lime juice and fish sauce, and toss and turn the noodles to incorporate the seasoning.

☐ Before serving, top the dish with bean sprouts, scallions and peanuts.

Like all noodle dishes, these are best served warm.

Thai Chicken Salad With Ramen Noodles

Ingredients

- 6 ounces Ramen Noodles
- 2½ pounds Rotisserie Chicken
- 4 cups Water
- ¾ cup Coconut Milk
- ¼ cup Lime Juice
- ¾ cup Reduced Fat Creamy Peanut Butter
- ¾ teaspoon Salt
- 1 tablespoon Sugar
- 1 small sized Cucumber
- ¼ teaspoon Cayenne

- 6 trimmed & thinly sliced Scallions
- ¼ cup chopped Fresh Cilantro

Instructions

☐ To start, peel the cucumber and remove all the seeds from it. Cut it into half lengthwise and then slice it into ¼ inch slices.

☐ Remove the skin of the chicken, and cut the meat into pieces.

☐ Boil water in a saucepan and, breaking the noodle cake into 4 pieces, add them to the water.

☐ When boiled, remove the saucepan from heat and cover it.

☐ In a large bowl, combine coconut milk, peanut butter, cayenne, salt, sugar, lime juice and cilantro, and blend well. Next, add chicken, cucumber and scallions to the bowl.

☐ Drain the water from the boiled noodles and rinse with cold water.

☐ Mix the noodles with the chicken mixture and toss to coat well.

The dish is best served steaming!

Broccoli And Ramen Noodle Salad

Ingredients
- 6 ounces Chicken Ramen Noodles
- 16 ounces Broccoli Coleslaw Mix
- ¼ cup Vegetable Oil
- 1/3 cup Cider Vinegar
- 1 cup Sunflower Seeds
- 1 cup Unsalted Peanuts
- ½ cup White Sugar
- A bunch of chopped Green Onions

Instructions

☐ Taking water in a boiling pot, let boil and add noodle cakes.

☐ When they are tender and easy to break apart, drain the water from the noodles and run under cold water. Toss them with a bit of olive oil to prevent them sticking with each other.

☐ In a large bowl, put the cooked noodles, green onions and coleslaw. Toss the ingredients together.

☐In a separate bowl, combine vegetable oil, sugar and the seasoning that came with the noodles. Stir this well and ladle it over the noodles evenly.
☐Toss the noodle mixture once again and refrigerate it until it is chilled.
☐When you want to eat it, remove it from the fridge and garnish with peanuts and seeds.

Ramen Beef Pie

Ingredients

- 2 packets Ramen Noodles
- 1 pound ground Beef
- 1/3 cup Vegetable Oil
- 2 cups Water
- ½ cup Onions
- A can of Sweet Corn

Instructions

☐ Pour the water in a pot and bring to a boil.

☐ When it starts boiling, add the noodle cakes to the water and cook for 2-3 minutes until the noodles become tender and start to break away.

☐ Drain the water from the noodles and run them under cold water.

☐ In a cooking pan, heat the vegetable oil. Fry the onions in the pan until they are browned.

☐ Cook the ground beef in the pan until it turns a deep brown color. Check that the beef is cooked completely; if not, let it cook a little more.

☐ Put the cooked beef in a pot which may fit in your oven.
☐ Ladle the sweet corns on top of the beef, followed by the cooked ramen noodles.
☐ Bake the dish for 10-15 minutes in the oven.
☐ When cooked, remove the pot from the oven and be ready to enjoy your special dish.

Chicken Ramen Diablo

Ingredients
- 1 packet Chicken Ramen Noodles
- 1 Chicken Breast
- 2 tablespoons Flour
- 1 tablespoon Vinegar
- 2 tablespoons Margarine
- ¼ teaspoon Thyme Leaves
- ¼ teaspoon Tarragon Leaves
- 1 tablespoon snipped Parsley
- 2 tablespoons chopped Onion
- 3 cups Water

Instructions

☐ Pour the water in a pot and bring to a boil.

☐ When it starts boiling, add the noodle cakes to the water and cook for 2-3 minutes until the noodles become tender and start to break away.

☐ Drain the water from the noodles and run them under cold water.

☐ Cook the chicken in a frying pan until it turns a nice brown color.

☐ Heat margarine in a saucepan on low heat, until it becomes golden brown.

☐ Add flour to the margarine and stir well.

☐ Remove the saucepan from heat and add water, seasoning dissolved in water, parsley, thyme, and tarragon leaves.

☐ Place the saucepan back on the heat and cook the mixture until it starts to boil, stirring frequently.
☐ When the mixture is done, transfer the ramen noodles to a serving bowl and top with the fried chicken and the prepared sauce.

This is a recipe that should not be kept waiting!

Fried Ice Cream Ramen

Ingredients
- 1 packet finely crushed Ramen Noodles
- 8 scoops Vanilla Ice cream
- 4 tablespoons Chocolate Syrup
- 2 tablespoons Butter
- ½ cup Honey
- ¼ cup Almonds
- Whipped Cream

Instructions

☐ Place a small skillet over medium heat and put butter in it.

☐ When the butter starts to melt, add the dry crushed ramen noodles into the skillet.

☐ Stir and sauté the ramen noodles until they are light brown in color.

☐ Turn the heat down a notch, and pour in honey, stirring the mixture until it dissolves completely.

☐ When the mixture in the skillet starts to bubble, add chopped almonds.

☐ Taking 2 scoops each of the ice cream in different bowls, ladle scoops of your prepared mixture onto the ice cream and serve for everyone to enjoy!

Raman Lasagna

Ingredients

- 6 packets Ramen Noodles
- 1 pound Italian Sausage
- 58 ounces Tomato Sauce
- 12 ounces Tomato Paste
- 2 teaspoons Garlic Powder
- 2 cups grated Mozzarella Cheese
- 23 ounces Ricotta Cheese
- 2 tablespoons dried Onion
- 1 tablespoon dried Parsley
- 1 tablespoon dried Oregano
- 1 tablespoon Salt
- 1 tablespoon Pepper

Instructions

☐ In a large bowl, combine tomato sauce, tomato paste, garlic powder, pepper, salt, onion, oregano and parsley, and stir until the mixture becomes one and there are no lumps.

- ☐ Remove the skin off the Italian sausage and cook it in a frying pan on medium high heat until it gives a deep brown color.
- ☐ Grease the base of a baking dish with some tomato sauce.
- ☐ Boil water in a pot and place the noodle cake in it. Cook the noodles until they can be separated easily. Do this with all the noodle cakes.
- ☐ Transfer the noodles onto a plate with a spatula, and also scoop out the sauce on top of the noodles.
- ☐ Pour ricotta cheese on top of the noodles, followed by the cooked Italian sausage.
- ☐ Drizzle the remaining tomato sauce on the sausages, and follow up with the other noodles.
- ☐ In the end, place a layer of Mozzarella cheese on top of the whole construction, and send the dish to the oven.
- ☐ Bake in the oven at 350 degrees for 40-45 minutes, or until the whole mixture is a deep brown color.

This recipe may seem lengthy, but the end result will leave you craving for more!

With this we come to the end of our chapter on ramen noodles. There is little doubt that you will enjoy making all the recipes listed above.

Soba Noodles

Soba noodles are one of the most versatile types of noodles to emerge from East Asia. Hugely popular in Japan, Soba noodles are made from buckwheat flour. They can be used equally effectively in hot and cold dishes. Plus, you can add them to soups or combine them with dipping sauce to create a unique delicacy.

Tempura soba is perhaps the most popular dish made using soba noodles. Yet, it can be said that there is no limit to the number of noodle recipes you can try at home using cooked soba noodles. There aren't any special methods and instructions you need to follow. Simply follow the instructions provided on the package and you are good to go.

Shrimp And Asparagus

Ingredients

- 6 ounces uncooked Soba Noodles
- 1 pound large sized Shrimp

- 2 cups diagonally cut Asparagus
- 1 tablespoon Peanut Butter
- 2/3 cup Fat Free Chicken Broth
- 1 tablespoon Vegetable Oil
- ½ teaspoon Dark Sesame Oil
- 2 teaspoons Sugar
- 2 tablespoons Rice Vinegar
- 2 tablespoons Soy Sauce
- ¼ cup thinly sliced Green Onions
- 1 teaspoon bottled minced Garlic
- 1 teaspoon bottled minced Fresh Ginger

Instructions

☐ Before starting with the rest of the recipe, peel and remove the veins from the shrimp, cleaning it well.

☐ Cook the noodles according to the instructions provided on the packet, but do not add fat and salt to the noodles.

☐ When the noodles are cooking, take chicken broth in a large bowl and add rice vinegar, soy sauce, peanut butter, sugar, ginger and sesame oil to the bowl. Stir the contents to ensure proper mixing.

☐ Place a nonstick skillet over medium-high heat and warm vegetable oil in it.

☐ Add garlic and sauté for 45 seconds. Next, add asparagus and cook for another 2 minutes.

☐ Next, add shrimp to the skillet and sauté for 2-3 minutes only.

☐ Place onions and the broth mixture to the skillet and cook until all the mixture becomes heated.

☐ When heated, add noodles to the mixture and toss to mix the ingredients well.
☐ Transfer the noodles to a serving bowl and eat away!

Otsu

Ingredients

- 12 ounces dried Soba Noodles
- 12 ounces Extra Firm Nigari Tofu
- 2 tablespoons Extra Virgin Olive Oil
- 2 tablespoons toasted Almond Oil
- ¼ cup Brown Rice Vinegar
- 1 tablespoon Honey
- 1 tablespoon Lemon Juice
- Zest of 1 Lemon
- 1/3 cup Shoyu Sauce
- 3 thinly sliced Green Onions
- ½ Cucumber
- ¼ cup toasted Sesame Seeds
- Peeled & grated Fresh Ginger
- ¼ cup chopped Fresh Cilantro
- ¾ teaspoon Fine Grain Sea Salt
- ¾ teaspoon Cayenne

Instructions
☐ Firstly, peel and remove the seeds from the cucumber. Cut it into half and then divide into ¼ inch slices.
☐ In a food processor, pour honey, cayenne, ginger, zest and salt and process until a smooth mixture is formed.
☐ Add shoyu sauce, lemon juice and vinegar to the mixture and start the food processor. While it is running, add the oils.
☐ Taking plenty of salted boiled water in a pan, place the noodles into the water and let cook until tender.
☐ When the noodles are tenderized, drain the water from them and rinse under cold water.
☐ Rinse the tofu, pat it dry with a paper towel and cut into tiny rectangles.
☐ Cook the tofu in a skillet over medium high heat, turning to cook evenly on both sides. When the tofu turns golden in color, remove it from the skillet.
☐ Taking a large bowl, mix together the noodles, cilantro, cucumber, onions and the mixture that you put together in the food processor.
☐ Toss the noodles to coat them well with the other ingredients. Add tofu to the mixture and toss once again.
☐ Garnish the noodles with sesame seeds and serve on a platter, all steaming hot!

Cilantro Noodle Bowl

Ingredients

- 8 ounces dried Soba Noodles
- 12 ounces Extra Firm Nigari Tofu
- ½ cup Extra Virgin Olive Oil
- Zest of 1 Lemon
- 2 large Garlic cloves
- 3 cups Broccoli
- 2 cups fresh Cilantro
- ½ teaspoon Fine Grain Sea Salt
- ¼ teaspoon Cayenne Powder

Instructions

☐ Boil water in a large pot and add salt to it. Place the noodle cakes in the water and let boil until tender.

☐ Before the noodles are fully cooked, add broccoli to the pot and let cook for another few seconds.

☐ Next, drain the noodles and rinse them with cold water. Sprinkle lemon zest on the noodles and set aside.

☐ Rinse and drain the tofu, and pat it dry. Cut it into small rectangles and cook it into a skillet over medium-high heat. When the pieces are browned, toss the tofu to cook on both sides.
☐ In a large bowl, mix together the noodles, broccoli and cilantro and toss the mixture to coat well.
☐ Add tofu to the noodle mixture and toss once again, mixing the ingredients well.
☐ Turn out the dish on to a platter, garnish with cayenne powder and sprinkle lemon juice on top before serving.

Ottolenghi Soba Noodles With Aubergine And Mango

Ingredients

- 8 ounces dried Soba Noodles
- 1 medium sized Aubergine
- 1 large ripe Mango
- 8 ounces grilled & cubed Tofu
- 1/3 cup Olive Oil
- 1 tablespoon toasted Coconut Oil
- Grated zest of 1 Lime
- Juice of 1 Lime
- ½ cup Brown Rice Vinegar
- ½ medium sized Red Onion
- ½ teaspoon Fine Grain Sea Salt
- 1/3 cup Fine Grain Natural Cane Sugar
- ¼ teaspoon Red Pepper Flakes
- A handful of slivered Basil Leaves
- A handful of chopped fresh Coriander
- 2 Garlic Cloves

Instructions
☐ Place a pot of water on heat to boil.
☐ Meanwhile, cook a mixture of salt, sugar and vinegar in a saucepan over medium heat. Stir the mixture until the sugar dissolves.
☐ Remove the vinegar mixture from heat and add sesame oil, pepper flakes and garlic.
☐ When the mixture cools down, add the lemon juice and zest to the saucepan.
☐ Placing a large skillet over medium heat, shallow fry the aubergine in sunflower oil until it turns golden. Transfer to a paper towel clad plate and sprinkle salt on top.
☐ Cook the noodles as written on the packet and, once cooked, drain and rinse them under cold water. Pour a slight trace of olive oil and toss the noodles to prevent them from sticking to each other.
☐ Place the noodles in a large bowl and add the vinegar mixture, aubergine, mango, tofu, onions, coriander and basil leaves, and toss the mixture very well.
☐ Set the dish aside for at least two hours, then warm and serve.

Curried Noodle Patties

Ingredients

- 4 cups cold Soba Noodles
- 6 ounces diced Tofu
- 4 Eggs
- 2 teaspoons Thai Curry Paste
- 2 tablespoons Olive Oil
- ½ teaspoon Sea Salt
- 6 chopped Green Onions
- ½ cup chopped Cilantro

Instructions

☐ Take a medium sized bowl and spread the curry paste at its base.

☐ Add one egg to the bowl and stir until the two are incorporated.

☐ Whisk in the other eggs, followed by tofu, salt, onions and cilantro.

☐ Now add the noodles into the paste. Place a skillet over medium heat.

☐ Pour 1/3 cup of the egg mixture into egg rings and cook for 3-6 minutes on each side until the color is golden brown. Cook the rest of the mixture in the same way.
☐ Sprinkle salt and pepper on the patties and eat away while they're hot!

Cold Soba Noodles

Ingredients

- 12 ounces dried Soba Noodles
- 12 ounces Extra Firm Tofu
- 7 tablespoons Olive Oil
- 1/3 cup toasted Pine Nuts
- 1 peeled & match-sized Radish
- 2 tablespoons grated & peeled Ginger
- 4 thinly sliced Scallions
- 5 medium sized, peeled & thinly sliced Shallots
- 1 bunch of minced Chives
- 1 teaspoon Fine Grain Sea Salt

Instructions
☐ Let water boil in a large pot.
☐ Meanwhile, pestle shallots, ginger and scallions in a mortar. Sprinkle salt on the crushed mixture and pestle a little more.

☐ Heat oil in a small saucepan and, when heated, transfer the shallot mixture to the pan and stir well. Transfer the mixture to a jar.

☐ Drain and dry the tofu, and cut it into ½ inch cubes.

☐ Place the skillet over medium-high heat and cook the tofu in it, until the pieces are browned on each side.

☐ Add salt to the boiling water, and prepare the soba noodles as per the instructions on the packet.

☐ Drain and rinse the noodles under cold water, and toss them with a bit of the oil to avoid sticking.

☐ Your dish is ready. Simply serve the noodles with the shallot paste, topped with chives, pine nuts and radish.

Grilled Tofu & Soba Noodles

Ingredients

- 12 ounces dried Soba Noodles
- 16 ounces drained Extra Firm Tofu
- 1 cup Extra Virgin Olive Oil
- 2 teaspoons fresh Lime Juice
- 1 teaspoon Natural Cane Sugar
- 3 medium Garlic Cloves
- 3 medium Shallots
- 1 bunch of Cilantro
- 3 small minced Serrano Peppers
- ¾ teaspoon Fine Grain Sea Salt

Instructions

☐ Boil a large pot of water, gradually adding salt to it.

☐ Cook the soba noodles in the boiling water, as per packet instructions.

☐ Drain the noodles and run them under cold water, tossing them with olive oil to prevent the stickiness. Place the noodles in a plastic bag and refrigerate.

☐ Using a mortar, pestle salt and garlic together into a paste, and then keep adding shallots one at a time, followed by the peppers.
☐ In the end, add the cilantro a handful at a time, and pestle the mixture to make it smooth.
☐ Next, add sugar, lime juice and olive oil to the smooth paste, and mix well until incorporated.
☐ Cut the tofu into slabs and coat them with olive oil.
☐ Placing the tofu slabs on a grill on medium heat. Cook on both sides until golden.
☐ To serve, transfer the soba noodles into a serving bowl and toss it with the dressing.

Almond Soba Noodles

Ingredients

- 12 ounces dried Soba Noodles
- 12 ounces Extra Firm Nigari Tofu
- 8 tablespoons Hot Water
- 2 tablespoons fresh Lemon Juice
- 2 teaspoons Red Curry Paste
- 12 slivered fresh Basil Leaves
- 1/3 cup Unsalted Almond Butter
- 4 ounces Pea Shoots
- ½ teaspoon Salt
- ¼ cup toasted & sliced Almonds

Instructions

☐ In a large bowl, mix the almond butter and curry paste, followed by lemon juice and salt.

☐ Pour hot water one tablespoon at a time, and keep stirring the mixture until it resembles a heavy cream.

☐ Cook the soba noodles in a pot of salted boiling water as per packet instructions.
☐ Drain and run the noodles under cold water, tossing them in olive oil to prevent them sticking to each other.
☐ Drain and dry the tofu while the noodles are cooking. Cut the tofu into small strips of ½ inch each.
☐ Placing a skillet over medium-high heat, cook the tofu strips on each side until they turn golden.
☐ In the very end of the cooking, add pea shoots to the skillet.
☐ In a separate bowl, combine the noodles with 2/3 the almond butter. Toss to mix the noodles with the other ingredients.

To serve your dish, place the noodles in a serving dish, drizzle with the remaining almond mixture, and garnish with almonds and basil.

Garlic Soba Noodles

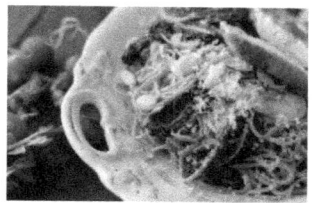

Ingredients
- 8 ounces dried Soba Noodles
- 12 ounces Extra Firm Tofu
- 2 lightly beaten Eggs
- Olive Oil, as needed
- ¾ cup freshly grated Parmesan
- 4 handfuls of destemmed & bite-sized Spinach
- A bunch of thinly sliced Green Onions
- ¾ cup Breadcrumbs
- A pinch of Salt
- 1 teaspoon Garlic Powder
- A handful of sliced Baby Radishes

Instructions
☐ Boil water in a pot and place the noodle cakes into it.
☐ Prepare the noodles as per the instructions provided on the noodle packet. Salt the water if you like.
☐ Drain the noodles and set them aside.

☐ During the preparation of the noodles, mix parmesan, breadcrumbs and salt in a bowl and stir until a paste appears.

☐ Cut the tofu into 6 equally sized rectangles, coat each piece with egg and then with the parmesan mixture.

☐ Line a baking sheet with brown paper and place the prepared tofu pieces onto it.

☐ Bake the dish in an oven at 375 degrees until both sides turn a golden color. When done, remove from the oven and slice into thin strips.

☐ Heat the olive oil in a skillet over medium high heat, and put in spinach and green onions, cooking for 2-3 minutes.

☐ Then add the cooked noodles, followed by parmesan and garlic powder. When these dissolve completely, remove the skillet from heat.

☐ Garnish the noodles with sprinkled radishes and serve with tofu slices on top.

Ginger Soba Noodles

Ingredients
- 12 ounces dried Soba Noodles
- 3 handfuls of baked Tofu
- 3 tablespoons chopped Tarragon
- 1 tablespoon freshly grated Ginger
- 1 teaspoon Mirin
- 3 tablespoons Brown Rice Vinegar
- ½ cup chopped White Onion
- 1 chopped Celery Stalk
- 1/3 cup toasted Squash Seeds
- 1 teaspoon toasted Sesame Oil
- 1/3 cup untoasted Sesame Oil
- Zest of ½ Lemon
- Juice of ½ Lemon
- ½ teaspoon Salt
- 2 teaspoons Brown Sugar

Instructions
☐ Cook the noodles as per packet instructions in salted water.

☐ Drain off the water, and rinse the noodles under cold water.

☐ While the noodles are cooking, put lemon zest and juice, onion, salt, sugar, mirin, celery, vinegar, ginger, toasted and untoasted sesame oil and onion in a food processor and blend until the concoction is very smooth in texture.

☐ Taking the prepared noodles in a large bowl, add tarragon, tofu, seeds and two thirds of the dressing to the bowl and toss the noodles to mix the ingredients.

☐ Your noodle recipe is ready. Simply pour into a plate and gobble it up!

Peanut Noodle Salad

Ingredients
- 18 ounces Soba Noodles
- 12 ounces Extra Firm Tofu
- ½ cup Hot Water
- ¼ cup Brown Rice Vinegar
- ¾ cup Creamy Peanut Butter
- 1 teaspoon Toasted Sesame Oil
- 2 crushed and chopped Garlic Cloves
- A pinch of crushed Red Pepper Flakes
- ½ cup Peanuts
- A bunch of thinly sliced Spring Onions
- A bunch of Asparagus Spears

Instructions
☐Place water in a pot to be boiled. When boiled, place the noodle cakes into the water and cook as per packet instructions.

☐ In the final stages of completion, add asparagus to the pot and let finish. Drain water from the noodles and run under cold water for a minute.

☐ In a medium bowl, combine peanut butter, sesame oil, garlic , red pepper flakes, rice vinegar and salt, and add hot water on top. Mix the ingredients well until incorporated into the water.

☐ Place the noodles in a serving dish and top with peanuts, asparagus and spring onions. Next, ladle the peanut butter mixture on top of the noodles before serving.

This brings us to the end of our noodle cookbook. Try these soba noodle recipes and discover flavor and taste you may not have experienced before.

Noodle Recipes

Simple Fried Noodles

Ingredients
- 1 pack of egg noodles, boil, then drain
- 2 sausages, round slices
- 3 tablespoons sweet soy sauce
- 1 tablespoon of soy sauce
- Salt to taste
- Pepper to taste
- Flavor taste
- 2 tablespoons of cooking oil
- 1 tomato, sliced
- 1 stem of leeks, sliced
- 3 red onion slices, sliced
- 2 cloves of garlic, sliced

How to make

1. Saute the slices until fragrant.
2. Enter the sausage slices, stir a little water, then add salt, pepper and flavoring to taste. Cook until fragrant.
3. Add the drained noodles, then give sweet soy sauce and soy sauce. Stir until the spices are absorbed.
4. Lift and serve

Spicy Fried Noodles

Ingredients
- 500 grams of wet yellow noodles
- 2 eggs
- 1 bunch of mustard greens
- 10 small size meatballs, cut into 4 parts
- 3 sausages, round slices
- 2 stems of leeks
- Chicken stock to taste
- 2 tablespoons of sweet soy sauce
- Right amount of oil
- 400 ml of water

Softened seasoning

- 3 grains of garlic
- 5 shallots
- Salt to taste

- Pepper to taste
- Cayenne according to taste

How to make

1. Heat cooking oil in a skillet. Add the eggs to stir roughly, then enter the noodles, the spices that have been mashed, mustard greens, leeks, meatballs, sausages, and stir again until evenly mixed.
2. Pour water, then add soy sauce and chicken broth. Stir again until blended and the spices soak.
3. Lift and ready to serve.

Jawa Fried Noodle

Ingredients
- 100 grams of dried egg noodles
- 100 grams of chicken meat, diced
- 2 carrots, sliced like a matchstick
- 100 grams of cabbage, sliced roughly
- 1 stalk of leeks
- 1 stalk of celery leaves
- 50 ml of water
- Right amount of oil
- 3 garlic cloves
- 1 clove of shallots
- 1/2 suing medium sized onion, thinly sliced
- 6 red chilies, sliced sliced
- ½ teaspoon of pepper powder
- 3 tablespoons of sweet soy sauce
- 1 tablespoon of soy sauce
- Salt to taste

- Flavor taste

How to make

1. Boil the noodles until cooked, remove and drain
2. Heat cooking oil, sauté garlic, onion and onion until fragrant.
3. Enter the chicken meat, stir until the spices soak.
4. Put the spring onions, carrots, cabbage and other spices, give water, cover the pan and let the spices soak. Then enter the noodles, stir again until they are evenly mixed and cooked.
5. Lift and serve with sliced celery and fried shallots.

Aceh Fried Noodle

Ingredients

- 500 grams of wet yellow noodles
- 750 grams of beef broth
- 150 grams of beef, cut into cubes
- 150 grams of shrimp, remove the skin
- 1 tomato, cut into cubes
- 4 cloves of garlic, sliced
- 3 red onion cloves, sliced
- 50 grams of bean sprouts
- 100 grams of cabbage, sliced roughly
- 1 teaspoons of vinegar
- 2 tablespoons of sweet soy sauce
- 1 stem of leeks, sliced
- 1 stalk of celery leaves
- Fried chips
- Pickled cucumber
- Salt to taste

- Right amount of oil

Softened seasoning

- 3 garlic cloves
- 2 Spring onions
- Chili according to taste
- 1 teaspoon turmeric powder
- 4 grains of cardamom
- 1 teaspoon cumin, roasted
- 1 teaspoon pepper

How to make

1. Heat oil, saute onion and garlic and mashed spices until fragrant. Add the meat, stir, until the meat changes color. Then add the shrimp and stir again until blended.
2. Add the broth, celery, chives, cabbage, bean sprouts, salt and vinegar, mix well.
3. Enter the noodles and sweet soy sauce. Mix well until cooked and the spices soak.
4. Lift and serve with fried chips and pickled cucumber.

Bandung Kocok Noodles

Ingredients

- 500 grams of boiled egg noodles
- 1 leg of cow
- 250 grams of bean sprouts
- 2 bay leaves
- 3 orange leaves
- 3 cm of ginger
- 2 cloves of shallots, mashed
- 3 garlic cloves, mashed
- Pepper to taste
- Salt to taste
- Adequate sugar
- Right amount of oil
- Enough water

Supplementary Ingredients

- Fried onion to taste

- Sliced chives to taste
- Cut enough celery
- Lime slices
- chili sauce

How to make

1. Boil the cow's legs until tender in the pan. Lift and drain. Then cut according to taste and put it back into the cooking water.
2. Heat cooking oil. Stir-fry the red onion and the garlic until you can smell the scent. Lift it and put it in a beef leg stew pan. Mix well.
3. Add ginger, orange leaves, bay leaves, salt, sugar and pepper. Mix well and cook again until boiling.
4. Arrange boiled noodles in the serving bowl with bean sprouts. Give the leg pieces of seasoned beef, then flush with the sauce. Give a sprinkling of shallots, chives, slices of celery, slices of lime and chili sauce.
5. Serve it.

Celor Palembang Noodles

Ingredients
- 500 grams of yellow noodles
- 100 grams of shrimp
- 100 grams of bean sprouts
- 200 ml of coconut milk
- 500 ml of water
- 1 teaspoon of salt
- ½ tablespoon of sugar
- 1/2 teaspoon of mushroom broth
- 2 stems of leeks
- 2 boiled eggs

Softened seasoning

- 4 cloves garlic
- 3 red onion cloves
- 1 tablespoon of dried ebi
- 3 red chilies
- 1/2 tablespoon of pepper
- 2 pecan nuts

How to make

1. Boil shrimp. Lift and set aside, take the broth.
2. Saute the spices until fragrant, add the shrimp and cook until it changes color.
3. Enter the broth / boiled water of shrimp and coconut milk. Cook until boiling.
4. Add cooked noodles until cooked, remove and drain water
5. Arrange noodles on a plate or bowl. Give bean sprouts on top and then pour with coconut milk sauce. Give egg slices and a sprinkling of celery or scallions and fried onions.
6. Serve it

Bogor Soto Noodles

Ingredients

- 150 grams of wet yellow noodles
- 50 grams of vermicelli, soak hot water, drain
- 250 grams of beef
- 100 grams of beef kikil
- 4 cloves garlic
- 3 red onion cloves
- 1 bar lemongrass, bruised
- 3 cm of ginger, crushed
- 3 cm galangal, bruised
- 2 orange leaves
- ½ teaspoon pepper powder
- Salt to taste
- Adequate sugar
- 1 liter of air
- Right amount of oil
- 50 grams of cabbage, sliced roughly

- 2 tomatoes
- 3 risol filled with vermicelli, fried then sliced
- 1 leek, iris
- 1 stalk of celery, sliced
- 1 tablespoon of fried onion

How to make

1. Boil the gravel until tender. Lift and drain. Cut to taste
2. Boil the meat until tender. Remove the meat and drain. Cut the meat according to taste. Take the cooking water.
3. Heat the oil. Saute the garlic and onion until fragrant. Lift and pour stir-fry into the meat stew pan.
4. Reheat the cooking water, then add lemongrass, galangal, ginger, orange leaves, salt, sugar, and pepper. Stir well.
5. Arrange yellow noodles and vermicelli in a serving container. Give cabbage, tomatoes, risol, chunks of meat and chopped chives, chives, celery, and fried onions. Flush with gravy.

Cakalang Manado Noodles

Ingredients
- 200 grams of egg noodles
- 150 grams of green mustard, cut into small pieces
- 100 grams of skipjack, shredded
- 2 stems of leeks
- 2 tablespoon of fried shallots

Gravy ingredients

- 4 cloves of garlic, finely chopped
- 2 tablespoons of cooking oil
- 1 ¼ teaspoon of salt
- ½ teaspoon pepper powder
- 1 liter of water

Vinegar chili ingredients

- 5 red chilies
- 1 clove of garlic
- 3 tablespoons of broth water

- 1 tablespoon of vinegar
- Salt to taste

How to make

1. Boil the egg noodles, remove and drain. Then mix with 1 tablespoon of cooking oil so it doesn't stick.
2. Heat cooking oil, saute garlic, pepper and salt until fragrant. Add the sliced skipjack, with mustard greens and leeks. Mix well while pouring water, and wait for it to boil. Lift and set aside.
3. Make vinegar sauce by smoothing the garlic, red chili, pepper and salt. Pour the skipjack and vinegar broth then mix well.
4. Arrange the noodles in a bowl, sprinkle fried shallots and serve with skipjack vinegar broth.

Bangka Chicken Noodles

Ingredients
- 500 grams of wet noodles
- 200 grams of chicken, boiled and cut into boxes
- 4 stalks of mustard, cut into pieces
- 100 grams of bean sprouts
- 2 tablespoons British soy sauce
- 2 tablespoons oyster sauce
- 2 stems of leeks, sliced
- 3 tablespoon sweet soy sauce
- 1 tablespoon of soy sauce
- 100 ml of chicken oil
- Salt to taste
- Flavor taste

Ingredients for broth

- 1/2 kg of chicken bone
- ½ teaspoon pepper powder
- 1 minced garlic clove

- 1 tablespoon sliced chives
- 1 tsp salt
- 2 liters of water

How to make

1. Make the broth first. Prepare a pan, then boil chicken bones, minced garlic, salt, pepper powder, until the fragrant broth.
2. Heat cooking oil, saute garlic until fragrant. Add the chicken, stir until the spices soak. Add oyster sauce, English sauce, sweet soy sauce, soy sauce, and add flavoring. Stir until well blended. Lift and set aside.
3. Arrange the noodles in a bowl, give the spiced chicken, mustard greens, bean sprouts and leeks, then serve with the sauce.

Bangka Koba Noodles

Ingredients

- 200 grams of egg noodles
- 200 grams of tengiri fish
- 100 grams of bean sprouts
- 2 stems of leeks
- 1 stalk of celery leaves
- 1 lemon
- 1 tablespoon fried onion

Gravy ingredients
- Broth of fish stew
- 3 garlic cloves
- 2 cm of ginger
- Enough water

Sauce ingredients
- 1 tablespoon of sweet soy sauce
- 1 tablespoon of soy sauce
- 1 tablespoon of brown sugar
- ½ teaspoon of onion oil
- Salt to taste
- Enough water

Supplementary ingredients

- 200 grams of tengiri fish
- 3 garlic cloves
- 1/2 suing onion
- 1 tablespoon of sweet soy sauce
- 1/2 teaspoon of soy sauce
- ½ teaspoon of salt
- 1 teaspoon of pepper powder
- 1/2 teaspoon of chicken powder broth
- Sugar
- Right amount of oil
- Enough water

How to make
1. Make the sauce, boil the mackerel, garlic, and ginger, until cooked and bald. Lift and set aside.
2. Heat the cooking oil saute garlic and onion until fragrant. Add the fish, mix well. Add sweet soy sauce, oyster sauce, soy sauce, pepper, salt, chicken

powder broth, and sugar. Mix well, then add water, cook until done. Lift and set aside.
3. Mix all the ingredients of the sauce, mix well and set aside.
4. Arrange noodles, bean sprouts, spring onions and seasoned fish, then pour the fish sauce and sauce into it. Give slices of celery, lime and fried onions.

www.ingramcontent.com/pod-product-compliance
Lightning Source LLC
Chambersburg PA
CBHW071437070526
44578CB00001B/119